NEXT CITIES

Typo-logical Drift

Emerging Cities in China

Shiqiao Li and
Esther Lorenz

Contents

Foreword
Made (Only) in China

With an urban population surpassing 800 million, our next global cities are enormously impacted by Chinese urbanization, currently outpacing, by at least three times, the rate of European and American urbanization following the industrial revolution. As China's urban dwellers have increased from being less than 20% of the population in 1980 to over 60% today, we need to understand not only the catalytic political and economic reforms prompting this massive migration from rural to urban territories, but also the conditions leading to the specific form that the city has taken through this high-speed evolution. While many scholars have focused on China's globalization, its participation in world trade, and the influence of importing and exporting goods and expertise across the East-West divide, *Typological Drift* is unique in its exploration of the impact of Chinese culture on the development of a distinct set of urban typologies specific only to this region.

Two critical moves set the trajectory for Shiqiao Li's and Esther Lorenz's book. The first, is to illuminate China's response, often presented as a globalized urbanism with undue influence from the West, from within Chinese culture—its value-laden conceptual underpinnings, language system, and social structures—rather than from without. The second, is to consider the evolution of this response through a biological rather than urban model. The authors ingeniously draw upon the concept of genetic drift, the way in which chance events can drive unanticipated evolutionary patterns in species through the changing frequency of distinct hereditary characteristics as these occur through populations over time. Genetic drift as applied to the formation of cities can be responsible for suppressing certain urban phenotypes so that they disappear entirely, while enabling other, perhaps more rare urban configurations to emerge. The documentation of these configurations and the cultural conditions that engender their formation—referred to as "drift triggers"— are the primary focus of this book.

At first glance, the three drift triggers that organize this work—ten thousand things, figuration, and group action—seem to have an affinity with Borges's rendition of a certain Chinese encyclopedia, used by Foucault in *The Order of Things* to expose the limited logics of

Western taxonomies. The concept of "ten thousand things" makes evident not only how a non-metric idea of quantity becomes a generator of urban quality in the profusion of goods and activities in the world marketplace of Yiwu, but also how the immanence of things, the irreducibility of their figuration, and their material manifestation in the world—conditions intrinsic to Chinese culture and language—operate in direct opposition to the model of transcendence dominating Western thought since Plato. Yiwu's overwhelming display of commodities is an embodiment of the excesses of global consumer capitalism localized within a single international trade city, where architecture is reduced to an organizing device, an infinite series of hidden micro-frames overflowing with an abundance of objects—from clothing and cameras to car parts—made in specialized Chinese manufacturing cities.

Within China, this massive capital-driven enterprise extends to the scale of the city. Global tourist destinations recreated as full-scale urban replicas figure the city itself as a miniaturization of other worlds peddled as exotic commodities in their own right. Whether as reconstructed historic sites drawn from China or abroad—scenographic backdrops generated for filmmaking or real life—or fashioned as a collection of contemporary avant-garde architectural artifacts such as the 100 villas by 100 architects for a Mongolian desert, this multi-scaled catalog of things populating the Chinese landscape undermines Western distinctions by enabling the authentic and fantastic, the past and future, and the vastly different scales and geographies of the handheld object and the city to occupy the same tableaux, all in defiance of occidental logics and their laws of language and geometry. Although perhaps a far cry from the *Celestial Emporium* described by Borges, the originality of thought organizing this book combined with its extensive grounding in historical research and contemporary empirical analysis, provide us with a truly unique lens through which to think about the material and social systems driving our economies, and the highly nuanced relationship between an evolving culture and its burgeoning cities, constituting a distinctive form of urbanism that, despite all claims to the contrary, should be understood to be made only in China.

Ila Berman, *Next Cities* series editor
Dean and Edward E. Elson Professor
University of Virginia School of Architecture

Acknowledgments

This book is nourished by the generosity of institutions and people that in one unique way—stemming from the book's broad mix of history and theory with extensive field trips and workshops over a period of a decade—embodies the heartening spirit of public scholarship in the area of constructed environment. We are deeply grateful for the help we received, and we hope the resulting book will justify the good faith in the production of knowledge so selflessly demonstrated by institutions, colleagues, students, and the general public.

The care at the School of Architecture, University of Virginia, is multifaceted and nurturing, all the more so for a topic that is so distant from the urban realities of Charlottesville. Dean Ila Berman not only brought the book to the ambitious *Next Cities* series, but also sponsored the production of the book with generous funds. This book is supported by a grant from the East Asia Center of the University of Virginia through its director Dorothy Wong. We are deeply indebted to the unfailing support from the Weedon Foundation; Mary Pollock, Luke Pollock, and Tom Romer have injected a great sense of value to our research through support for the Weedon Professorship in Asian Architecture, the School's summer program in China, and for the exhibitions, lectures, and symposia associated with this research. Justin O'Jack, the endlessly resourceful director of the Shanghai Office of the University of Virginia, has given our research and teaching a foot in the territory in Shanghai. Handel Lee's love for cutting-edge architectural and urban research is manifested in his substantial support for the Weedon Professorship. Yunsheng Huang's foundational endeavor to establish a link with China, since 1993, is instrumental to the School's tradition of research in Chinese architecture. The librarians and technologists at the University of Virginia have guided us masterfully as we tread apprehensively in the world of complex possessions of data: GIS specialist of the Scholar's Lab Chris Gist, architectural librarian Rebecca Coleman, East Asia librarian Wei Wang, multimedia teaching and learning librarian Josh Thorud, and library counsel Brandon Butler.

At the germination of the project—in the form of research projects on China's "super practices" (architectural Design Institutes) and "central business districts"—was the support from the Research Grant

Council of the government of Hong Kong, the institutional support from the School of Architecture, The Chinese University of Hong Kong, and the collaboration of colleagues and students. Wang Ying rendered great assistance in background research and logistics. Nelson Chen, Doreen Heng Liu, Gordon Matthews, and Hendrik Tieben continued to share their insights into the makeup of the Chinese city. Colleagues at the School of Architecture, Southeast University, Li Hua, Ge Ming, and Chen Wei have in the past 15 years offered an infrastructure of research without which this book would not have been possible. These included international conferences on indigenous ideas of Asia, the planning of adventurous expeditions to parts of China rarely visited by urban researchers, and everything in between. It was their meticulous care for the intellectual and physical wellbeing—from heated discussions in air-tight conference rooms to elegant tea gatherings in beautiful gardens—that have sustained the research and teaching that ground the content of this book. At the School of Architecture, South China University of Technology, Peng Changxin, whose connection with the University of Virginia was cemented with a year-long visiting scholar position, has hosted us and our students in Guangzhou with a generosity beyond words. It is from this research base at the School of Architecture in Guangzhou that we launched our various research trips in the surrounding Pearl River Delta areas. At the School of Architecture, Hunan University, Wei Chunyu welcomed us with the open joy of a *literatus*; Lu Jiansong and Jiang Min gave us a memorable occasion, through a design workshop and field trips on the theme of the new Chinese village, to understand Chinese urbanization outside the two major delta areas of the Pearl River and the Yangtze River.

Closer to China's urban realities, it was the front-line leaders of design in architectural offices who gave us invaluable access and insight into the Chinese city: as a leading designer and thinker in contemporary Chinese architecture, Liu Xiaodu (Urbanus) has shared deep knowledge and firsthand experience of the complex realities of urbanization with us for over a decade. Liu Yichun (Atelier Deshaus) gave us thoughtful presentations explaining the cultural meanings behind his architecture. Wang Shu (Amateur Architecture Studio) moved us with his architecture and his delightful conversation. Philip Yuan (Archi-Union) illuminated our thoughts through an infectious radiance he brings to research and design. Over the years we have learned a great deal from many others to whom we are genuinely grateful: Zhang Ke (Standardarchitecture), Gary Chang (Edge Design), Bernard Lim (AD+RG), Humphrey Wong (Meta4), Eunice Seng, Koon Wee, and Darren Zhou (Skew Collaborative), Jasmine Tsoi and Chris Lai (DOffice), Rocco Yim and William Tam (Rocco Design Architects), Han Baoshan (Suzhou Institute of Architectural Design), Zhang Hua (Shanghai Xiandai Architectural Design Group), Liu Erming, Mao Xiaobing, Tongji Architectural Design Group (TJAD), Gensler Shanghai, and KPF Shanghai.

Students are engines of research; in 2015 and 2016 when our teaching in China was dedicated to the research on emerging city typologies in China, the participating students made an immense contribution to the book's theme. In 2015, students from the University of Virginia: Di Chen, Ismaelia Dejoie, Tamara Dennis, Stephanie Granados, Jacqui Kenyon, Xiaoshuo Lei, Yijun Li, Sangyoon Park, Donna Ryu, Seth Salcedo, Michelle Stein, Qintian Wang, Dillon Wilson, Sijia Zhang; students from Southeast University in Nanjing: Zhai Lian, Lu Xi, Chen Yiqian, Liu Yaokun, Jiang Wei, Zhang Yibo, Shao Xingyu, Li Yidan, Liu Xiaodan, Dong Yitong, Wang Jingshu, Wang Ren, Liu Zhaolong, Zhao Yuan, Wu Weiqiao. In 2016, students from University of Virginia: Meredith Blake, John Devine, Scott Getz, Rebecca Good, Meng Huang, Karilyn Johanesen, Boning Luo, McKenzie Rist, Shannon Ruhl; students from Southeast University in Nanjing: Huang Enze, Meng Zheng, Liu Tengxiao, Xing Yifan, Guo Yiwen, Yu Junwang, Ye Zhi, Han Yalan, Wang Qian.

Fieldwork is both exciting and at the mercy of circumstances; we are deeply grateful for the guides and drivers who not only took us to where we knew but also where we did not—both have great significance in our research. In Hangzhou, Shi Hongchao organized, often remotely, our complex site visits. In Shanghai, Dijia Chen enabled us to visit many leading architectural offices. In Hangzhou, Wu Yi, aka our "favorite driver," braved bad weather and dark nights to bring us to all kinds of strange locations with his consummate skill to maneuver his large and immaculately appointed bus. In Shanghai, Yang Hailong at the fabulous Astor House Hotel organized transportation for site visits for many years. In Hengdian, Zhu Teng of Hengdian Group gave us access to parks and film locations that we did not anticipate. Zheng Luting tirelessly explained the intersections between film sets, historical tales, tourism, and life, and Du Yingkai showed us the nascent real estate market. In Yiwu, trade agent Jack Li helped us navigate the ocean of commodities without which the consequences can be tragic. In Minmetals Hallstatt, Zhu Haoliang patiently showed us all residential unit types and their selling points. In Foshouhu, Nanjing, Li Xinyang explained to us the highlights of cutting-edge art and architecture. In Thames Town, Deng Cheng revealed to us Chinese homes behind British façades. In Huaxi, the Longxi Hotel driver went out of his way to invite us to his home and to show his transition from a farmer to a driver.

Our talented team of research assistants have brought the 60 or so drawings to very high standards. Donna Ryu and Meng Huang worked on early drafts of the book. Hutchins Landfair, with creativity, perseverance, commitment, and care, created many of the maps and axonometric drawings often from limited information. Zhou Sicheng contributed through his persistent resourcefulness in visualization. Cheng Chen's research into the basic data of Chinese urbanization filled several information gaps. Jiawei Chen, Shan Zhu, Xianwen Xu, Zimo Ren, Amelia Lin, and Ted Bazil have helped produce many of the splendid maps and axonometric drawings. Gu Xueping at South China University of Technology provided much-needed site photography and references. Neil Donnelly, Ben Fehrman-Lee, and Siiri Tännler gave us a privileged view of what a great graphic design looks like, imbuing a deeply appreciated depth to the visual impact of the book. Sneha Patel orchestrated the entire production process amidst all the demanding tasks as the communications director of the School of Architecture. The dedication of Jake Anderson at ORO Editions has greatly facilitated the progress of the book.

We are humbled by the collective efforts behind the book, and are invigorated by the documentation and tentative framing of urban realities, with all the vitality of their spatial and formal idiosyncrasies that seem to escape normative urban theory.

This book is dedicated to the memory of Li Zhongqian.

Shiqiao Li and Esther Lorenz
September 2020
Charlottesville

Introduction

The 659 million people who transitioned from being rural to being urban from 1978 to 2018 have pushed China's urban population to about 831 million and changed Chinese cities in distinctive ways. This development is unprecedented for the world. What is truly unique about this development is not the building of infrastructure, the construction of cities, the increase of economic production, the development of technologies, the creation of urban and rural populations, the rise of wealth and inequality, or even the sense of alienation and dislocation; these are normative narratives of urbanization and the mainstays of urban research. Nor is it about just scale and speed. Instead, what is truly unique are the forces of the Sinitic culture. Urbanization has been largely a discourse within Indo-European settlement patterns; this Sinitic development, even though influenced by Indo-European urbanization patterns, presents intriguing consequences that are yet to be understood culturally. Existing literature on China's urbanization touches on culture far too lightly, often perpetuating prejudices of seeing urbanization in China (and other parts of the world) as a European and American event gone rogue. The existing literature on culture, on the other hand, tends to overlook urbanization; perhaps it is too unsettling and new.

This book attempts to understand what culture does to city types, stressing the significance of understanding entirely different cultural foundations of the Sinitic civilization: in the meanings of distribution of things, in the visual underpinning of the Chinese language and its writing system, and in the social structures based on larger groups of individuals acting in coordination. These make up fundamentally different assumptions for cities, even though the eventual result bears some resemblance to Indo-European settlement patterns. In the context of world civilizations, the Sinitic civilization is largely independent and unique; it is impossible not to take this at its deepest level in any attempt to understand its artifacts. It is on this basis of the multi-polarity of cultures that this book contextualizes change: the global flows of people, money, goods, and materials go through "filters" of culture that change their natures. If typology remains a viable grip on the otherwise nebulous framing of cities, then what has solidified in cities in China gives us a new set of typological features. This book does not wish to perpetuate the duality of norms and aberrations of cities in relation to privacies and publics, freedoms and restrictions, haves and have nots; its first goal is to reset these norms and aberrations into productive divergences that are capable of both goodness and injustice. Alterity is always groundbreaking for the habitual; the design and construction of cities deserve to prosper in this context of productive divergences despite the complexity of the task.

This book presents thirteen case studies, each described with a map of urban context, an essay framing key cultural concepts, a "typological drift drawing" visualizing distinctive characters, and a series of analytical and documentary illustrations providing depictions in detail. Scales of these case studies vary considerably, from the embryonic to the fully flourished; it is, however, not the uniformity of scale but the promise of developmental propensity that guided the curatorial decisions of the book.

Drift of City Types

In documenting the effects of cultural filters on cities as enormous social, economic, and political constructs, we have intentionally mapped the framework of this book on models of biological evolution. The greatest limit of the biological evolution models for cities is that capitalism as our current driver for urbanization is defined by endless accumulation, while biological evolution models are defined by a dynamic equilibrium. The virtues of the book's modeling are also apparent: city types transform because of internal cultural change (mutation), external economic and environmental conditions (adaptation), and influx of new peoples (migration). The rise of Christianity as internal cultural change in the Roman Empire shifted common city types from forum- and game-centered public spaces to church-centered ones; while the Roman city had its origin in the Greek agora, the Christian city was rooted in the form of the new type of the monastery, giving rise to spaces of study and care (mutation). Nineteenth-century industrialization profoundly changed many cities economically from agricultural- and trade-based cities to manufacture-based cities with their intense demand for supply chains and mass labor (adaptation). Most European-looking cities in many parts of the world outside Europe are results of expansions of European peoples and cultures (migration). A history of cities would normally take into account all these developments. In this book, we aim to explain the rise and development of Chinese cities in the past four decades in terms of a fourth equally powerful if less predictable force: drift.

Drift of phenotypes takes place when unexpected events randomly terminate some features and allow other features to flourish; this process is unconnected with mutation, adaptation, and migration. In the past three decades, Chinese cities have indeed been results of several key cultural forces that effectively functioned as "unexpected events" in the normative process of globalization. People, money, goods, and materials moved in increasing speed and quantity around the world, yet they are uniquely shaped by a set of cultural forces in China as "drift triggers."

To understand drift we must first understand the likely urban process. Global urban expansion, in the past centuries since the Portuguese navigation in the 1500s, has been a European driven process; the trade routes Portugal established set a precedent for all the successive European empire builders to follow. Industrialization since the nineteenth century was a major boost for European global expansion; the idea of mass manufacturing of standardized goods and services demanded much larger amounts of resources to be secured worldwide. Neoliberalization since the late twentieth century broke down further the division of nations in search for cheaper raw materials and labor. For some time, this European and American model of urban expansion looked as if it would be the future: a form of the "end of history" as Francis Fukoyama called it. But, China's urban reality surprised us all.

To comprehend China's "drift triggers," we must understand, even if just in outline, what Chinese cities were like before their European and American peers descended on them with alienating features. Given the size and cultural diversity, perhaps no single typology can adequately describes "the Chinese city." What seems to be broadly consistent is that, since the Han dynasty (206 BCE to 200 CE), imperial Chinese cities have invested enormously in central control. This is materialized in both institutions and in space; the centrality of imperial palaces and its spaces of legitimation in the form of ancestral temples were by far the most dominant spaces and structures. In contrast, the marketplace kept a low profile; the idea of "equal exchange" of the marketplace—like the agora of the ancient Greeks—did not seem to serve the purpose of hierarchical central control. Max Weber argued that the single most distinctive feature of the "Occidental city," compared with the "Asiatic city" (primarily Chinese), is that they contain oath-bound political associations, armed citizenry, craft and merchant guilds, and city leagues; it is the political autonomy that defined the fundamental role of these institutions in cities.[1] Chinese cities, despite their fortifications, markets, and merchant associations, functioned in a power structure resembling a concentric circle, very different from the practice of the model of multiple autonomous power centers in European cities. The Mongol invasion in the eleventh and twelfth centuries (Song dynasty), and the European globalization resulting from colonization in the late seventeenth century (late Ming dynasty), brought some pressure on Chinese cities to adapt to the European model, but Chinese cities never changed their concentric political structure and the architecture that held it together. Prior to the late nineteenth century, one cannot say that the dominant typology of imperial Chinese cities changed with its acceptance of commerce;

rather, it tolerated it, even when China's commerce was by far the largest in the world in the seventeenth century. Rather than conferring political independence to the merchant class, imperial courts embarked on the production of orthodoxies: the Song dynasty's New Confucianism and Ming dynasty's obsession with reviving Han Chinese cultural standards. In the process, the merchant class was eager to portray themselves as *literati*, building sophisticated gardens to display their newly acquired cultivation. The *bourgeoisie* never emerged to demand their own city in China, unlike what happened in Europe. As a result, until the beginning of the nineteenth century, Chinese cities held onto an imperial city model, which was still sufficiently represented by the imperial Beijing, where central features of Chinese cities dating back to two thousand years ago were still present and functioning. Popular and vernacular urban cultures appeared only in periphery zones such as the southern part of Beijing (Qianmen), just outside the formidable gates of the Forbidden City. Up to this point, the Chinese city was unrelated to the idea of the *polis* of the Greeks, where politics, culture, and commerce played out in public space.

The one hundred years of the twentieth century changed all that. The turning point was the Opium War (1839–1842), which concluded with the British gaining trade access to China and territories in Hong Kong and Shanghai. With these territories, the British, followed closely by many other European powers, showcased the European city in China. The Chinese intellectual elite at the time was impressed, and a radical change in Chinese cities began that incorporated many features of European and American cities. Shanghai is a prime example; it flourished from the late nineteenth century to the middle of twentieth century, when the Second World War and a civil war in China ended with the Chinese Communist government taking over China. The new leaders were rural in their outlook and despised urban culture; they campaigned rigorously against the city and promoted, instead, the rootedness of rural life. This is not without precedents in China; the Ming dynasty in the fourteenth century also promoted the virtue of peasant life in the face of a perceived excessive foreign influence in the previous Mongol dominated Yuan dynasty. From 1950s to 1980s, Chinese cities went through a period of decline, while cities in the rest of the world grew tremendously riding on the rise of consumerism as the principal characteristics of the American century.

As if to mark a new century, in 2001, China became a member of the World Trade Organization (WTO). What led to the membership was the record of accomplishment of almost twenty years of an experiment, beginning in 1979, with a market economy under Deng Xiaoping's leadership. The West, led by the Clinton administration, was convinced that market reform would change China socially and politically into a regime more similar to those of the West. The neoliberalist marketplace in Europe, America, Japan, South Korea, Taiwan, Hong Kong, and Singapore also found a disciplined labor force and a country willing to forego its environmental quality to accommodate the search for greater profits. It was a perfect match. With the WTO membership, Chinese cities entered into the value chain of a global economy in full force, leading to the most spectacular urban development in the history of human settlement. China's urbanization rate increased from about 18 percent in 1978 to about 60 percent today, an increase in urban population of about 659 million.[2] If the Chinese nineteenth century was all about how to push foreign influences out of China, the first two decades of the twenty-first century was all about how to reach out to the rest of the world. To build the most advanced city has been for decades one of the most powerful motivations in Chinese urbanization. China became the new standard for the "developmental state" that strategized value creation through real estate and city building.[3] It looked like China was about to embrace the city as it was established in the European tradition. However, we have so far underestimated the strength of the Sinitic culture, which acted as triggers that produced typological drift in Chinese cities, comparable to the consequences of genetic drift. As much as Chinese cities are consequences of a global redistribution of the value chain, they are also creators of a new global capitalism following their own cultural logic. Chinese cities are the infrastructures of a Chinese economic and cultural life, which may or may not be framed as capitalist, and they have created a new urban reality.

Drift Triggers

A drift trigger, as we call it in this book, is otherwise known as either a bottleneck or a founder's effect; it is a restriction placed on the migration of phenotypes from one place to another, so that particular features, which are normally not dominant in the original ecology, become dominant under the new environmental conditions. Chinese cities can be seen as consequences of a set of very distinctive cultural "bottlenecks" in the history of city types. This book frames three most consequential ones: the notion of ten thousand things (*wanwu*), figuration, and the preference for group action, each propelling the Chinese city into directions that had not been possible in other cultural contexts.

Drift Trigger One: Ten Thousand Things

The idea of ten thousand things (*wanwu*)—a much more elegant expression in Chinese than in English—is a key intellectual framework in the Chinese cultural context. The "ten thousand" stands for "all"; it is a conventional way of describing the world through its "things" rather through its "principles." Plato, in *Timaeus*, suggests five abstract shapes to be the foundational components that make up all the diversity of the world through a well-proportioned mathematical structure. The conception of the world according to Plato, and to many subsequent European philosophers, is the idea that a simpler structure can be found to adequately "represent" the complex material reality, and this "represented reality" is a higher form of knowledge. This is the European epistemology. The genetic code, for instance, stands for the structure of life; this is both exhilarating and frustrating as life is contingent on much more than genetic codes. Architectural production, like other forms of cultural productions, is dominated by the search for the "just right" as its principle: "nothing could be added, diminished or altered, but for the worse," as Alberti phrased it. Excess, as in the baroque, is only possible as a transgression of the just right. This, as we will discuss later, is already foretold in the way the Greek alphabet works as a medium of language: a much smaller set of modules making up varieties of words. The Chinese intellectual framework does not work like this at all; it thinks through the true via the actualities of things—as many as necessary—instead of through the principles that represent them. This is "immanent" thought, as Marcel Granet speculated.[4] Higher forms of realities (including the divine) are largely absent from this framework, other than a vague sense of unity of humans and the natural world (the *Dao*, for instance). The difference between China and Greece cannot be more profound.[5]

The spectrum of consequences of this Chinese intellectual framework can be seen in both literati gardens and cities producing popular commercial products for the world. The literati garden—private gardens of the cultivated scholars with the highest social status in traditional China—is a carefully curated collection of all significant (thus beautiful) things: rocks, bamboo, plum trees, pine trees, water, water lilies, fish, birds, etc. These would blend with a vast number of Chinese characters, which, together with the garden, narrate the poetic beauty and confirm the natural orders of things. Here, the smallest number would be the reproductive *yin* and *yang*, rather than a mathematical truth. Chinese thought is always about autopoiesis so much so that it never had to name its absence. Thus the "minimalist" approach here would be grounded in this fertility principle arising from complementary opposites, and not on that of mechanical reproduction guided by mathematical principles, an aesthetic sensibility apparent in the paintings of Wen Zhengming (1470–1559) who witnessed the rise of literati gardens in the Ming dynasty.

Chinese popular culture, however, takes *wanwu* literally; here, the notion of good life is literally embodied in the profusion of goods.[6] In this context, less is less and more is more. The absence of moralization of quantity—such as proportionality and propriety in relation to quantities—legitimizes a world of goods without the guilt of excess. Ming dynasty novels are filled with endless enumerations of lists of goods (particularly silver pieces), using these lists of goods as real measures of the depth of awe, respect, gratitude, love, and lust.[7] Quantity in traditional political hierarchy was highly regulated to signify rankings of power; it is displayed through sizes and number of columns, bracket sets, roof ornaments, and words on buildings. Quantity is also an economic strategy; the production of good life is the production of the profusion of goods. The display of the profusion of goods is always present, perhaps most commonly experienced with an elaborate meal; food in abundant display contrasts with the measured proportionality of dishes and courses at a European dinner table. Human flourishing needs to be seen in the abundance of things.

China's popular love for ten thousand things enters into a strangely productive relationship with global capitalism in its endless pursuit of more with less. Since China became a member of the World Trade Organization, labor-intensive and high polluting industries moved to China with great haste, having found a hard-working, disciplined, and tolerant workforce and a government ready to make concessions. At the same time, China's cultural context added crucial momentum to the increasing scale and quantity of factories in China. With the arrival of foreign factories, China's own enterprises rose to compete with them in scale and cost. A race to the bottom through quantity ensued. The popular culture of ten thousand things is a key sentiment that provided this race to the bottom with a supportive cultural infrastructure.

The hard-working, disciplined, and tolerant labor force is, above all, the foundational condition in China. While the toil of labor has a universal impact on the biological bodies of humans, the way it is understood in different cultures makes a decisive difference. China's understanding of labor is far more sympathetic to the goals of global capitalism. Labor and the laboring body has been constructed in Europe to be lacking in meaning since ancient Greece. Karl Marx argued that regulated labor alienates human life; Hannah Arendt takes this point further to say that, while work is meaningful, labor is animalistic and demeaning to human life. A human makes; he/she does not labor. The result of making is something permanent, such as a code of law and a piece of art; the result of labor is fleeting and ephemeral, such as a single-use consumer product. The great consequence of labor is not just that it is ephemeral; it is the result of humans becoming thoughtless consumers subject to political manipulation. Arendt made a convincing interpretation of this history of slavery starting with the ancient Greeks; the Greeks made use of slaves not so much exclusively for economic gains but for the purpose of freeing Greek citizens from labor of subsistence. Only the medieval monastery broke with this tradition perhaps as a deliberate act against the Roman notion of human leisure and play (*otium ludens*); religious devotion and physical labor became one and the same (*ora et labora*). The eighteenth-century European *bourgeoisie* returned to "freedom from labor," institutionalizing slavery and class stratification in society to create a "culture of politeness" through manners and estates. Capitalism may have become saturated in Europe because the inherent cultural bias against the laboring body contained a limit of its economic use.

The Chinese conception of labor is very different. While in most European languages there are two separate words for labor and work, in Chinese, there is only one word, *lao*. Semantic richness often reflects on how language and culture conceive values; the Chinese culture does not seem to distinguish intellectual labor from physical labor in terms of social stratification. Instead, labor seems to be the same activity taking place in the mind or in the body: Mencius claimed that those, who rule, labor mentally and those, who are ruled, labor physically.[8] Labor of subsistence, such as in agriculture, has often been highly valued, as during the early years of the Ming dynasty when scholars and peasants were ranked higher than craftsmen and merchants. This general cultural acceptance of labor in China can easily be adapted to the division of labor of capitalism. When China experimented with a labor-intensive production base for foreign firms, young people flocked to factories with little hesitation; this is one of the most important cultural factors in the success of China's manufacturing capacity, the absence of cultural stigma of the laboring body. It makes labor specialization effective. It creates an extreme form of labor specialization that enables village and town enterprises to operate effectively to produce commodities in large quantities.

Drift Trigger Two: Figuration

What orders the world if not precise laws, principles, and formulas at a higher level, frequently represented by the anthropomorphic all-powerful supernatural beings? Instead of higher forms of knowledge (form, noumenon, ontology), Chinese thought sees the order of the world in the features and connections of the things of the world. The key to understand the order of the world is through the notion of the figure (*xiang*), as in ten thousand figures (*wanxiang*) to mean all things in order, and in sceneries of figures (*jingxiang*) to mean a condition (social, natural, aesthetic) to be comprehended.

Figure is form in an essentialized condition, but not a Platonic abstract Form, nor a linguistic sign. Figure does not exist outside its materiality; it is closer to an aura of a thing or an icon. Figures are both natural and artificial; the creation and integration of artificial figures are ways of making effective changes. The creation and integration of artificial figures can be understood as "figuration," the coming into existence of sceneries of figures. In the materiality of figures, Chinese thought remains inextricably linked to things, speaking the true always via material truthfulness. Each thing, instead of being considered as an iteration of an archetype, is seen to have its own reason; "ten thousand things all have their own principles, and it is easy to follow them but difficult to go against them," claimed the influential eleventh-century Confucian scholar Cheng Hao.[9] Furthermore, "outside Dao there are no things and outside things there is no Dao."[10] More importantly, values are advocated through figures. For instance, the uprightness and determination in human character are figuratively materialized in the uprightness of bamboo and defiance of the plum blossom in winter. The righteousness of life and human character is blended together in a complex web of figures—both natural and artificial—that give rise to the existential grounding of life. The artful assembly of figures produces a "propensity" (*shi*) that is always fluid, capturing the propensities of an existing condition through its figures and guiding it to its next stage with efficacy.[11] For instance, the calligrapher does not begin with a pre-determined sketch, but with a broad goal actualized through each brush stroke that carries the existing propensity from previous strokes and creates a new propensity for following strokes. From politics to art, this way of ordering life through strategies of figuration is key to understanding Chinese cultural production and urbanism. Living a meaningful life through immanent thought does not involve any notion of rule-giving supernatural beings; it is certainly a testament to the strength of figuration.

The robustness of figuration in the creation of meaning of life lies ultimately in the Chinese writing system, by far the most important component of the Chinese language. The Chinese writing system is what held the Sinitic civilization together for over 5,000 years despite nomadic invasions, internal uprisings, and natural disasters. Most languages in the world today (about 46 percent) are derived from Indo-European origins; the Sinitic languages (about 22 percent) form the next largest language family. Our world is unmistakably Indo-European. The single most important distinction between them is perhaps this: Indo-European languages are phonetic and Sinitic languages are visual. It is the case of the ear versus the eye. In establishing the academic field of linguistics, Ferdinand de Saussure was eager to proclaim that the study of language is the study of speech acts exclusively.[12] This "phono-centric" view of language is a feature deeply rooted in earlier Indo-European thought, in the notion of the divinity of breath in the *Rig Veda*, in the consideration of speech as the "essence of man" in the *Chandogya Upanishad*, and in the denigration of writing in Plato's *Phaedrus*. European philosophy is filled with this sense of intellectual superiority of the alphabet-based languages, from Francis Bacon and G. W. F. Hegel to Walter Ong, Eric Havelock, and William Hannas; they predicted that the Greek alphabet would eventually replace the Chinese characters. The decline of Egyptian hieroglyphics and the eradication of Mayan hieroglyphics are also consequences of what may be described as "phonetic imperialism." It is not surprising that Jacques Derrida focused on a "grammatology" in an attempt to unpack the inherent cultural strategies of privileging in the European tradition of knowledge production.

The most rudimentary understanding of the Chinese language is that it operates as a system of visual patterns, and not as a system of notations of sounds. This sets Chinese civilization into a very different direction. Sound making—and the phonetic sound notations—is an act of abstraction: acoustics does not resemble the thing, rather it signifies it. In complete contrast, the Chinese writing system begins with a visual likeness of the thing, a figure. It "reverse engineers" figures for meanings that do not have physical forms. What comes from this very first divide is the cultivation of two different sensibilities: the love of differentiations of sound, and the love of the fixity of the figure. The love of sound differentiation in language—grammar—takes us to synthetic constructs of complex systems of signifying structures relatively abstracted from the "signified." This complex structure has a deep impact on the formation of all cultural constructs; this is what makes structuralism such an influential conception. Writing of visual patterns derails this project of linguistics. The love of figures—the foundation of calligraphy as the highest art form in China—channels thoughts toward the centrality of essentializing visual forms in the world, delineating a complex network of figures that form the basis of a meaningful relationship between human life and everything else. For the Chinese mind, phonetic abstraction is deeply unsatisfying as the language takes the mind away from the object of its description, a philosophical frustration keenly observed by Leibniz who wished to invent a "universal character" similar to Chinese characters.

The European city is deeply influenced by versions of grammatical thinking applied to forms, while the Chinese city is organized through the deployment of figures. The ideas of shape grammar, pattern language, and space syntax are compelling frameworks of making and understanding cities and meanings in Europe and America, but they have little currency in China beyond academic circles. Instead, the craving of the Chinese culture is for figures that generate propensities poetically with ten thousand things; this is the comfort zone of Chinese moral and aesthetic life. As in any field of cultural production, one encounters "figuration" at all levels of accomplishments and for all economic and political goals.

While capable of achieving sophisticated elegance as evidenced in literati paintings and gardens, figuration's popular manifestation—from landscape gardens and skylines of cities—is perhaps the most astonishing to the eye. We observe figuration at work in the staging of political power and nationalism in important events such as 2008 Beijing Olympic games and 2010 Shanghai Expo. Beijing's grand figurative scheme of the square and the circle, fire (red) and water (blue) at its Olympic Park collaborated with the imperial scheme of the square and the circle, heaven and earth in the Temple of Heaven and the Altar of Agricultural Ancestors. Figuration is deeply embedded in the development of China's new towns. Real estate developers build figurated exotic or cutting-edge modern architecture embodying versions of good life to justify higher prices. The entertainment industry uses figurated ancient Chinese cities to attract tourists, film crews, and to offer stories from the past. Municipal and provincial governments deploy figurated modernity in their central business districts, science and technology parks, and eco cities to manifest power and status relative to central government. Larger narratives of nationalism and good life are composed based on this plethora of figurative constructions.

Drift Trigger Three: Group Action

Unlike Aristotle who believed that family could never produce justice and truth (*Politics*), Confucius thought that family is the archetype of human society (*Lunyu*); according to Confucius, human societies are naturally hierarchical like that of the family: kings and ministers, fathers and sons are modeled on the same relational reality. The key to avoid oppression and violence is not to abandon the hierarchical structure of the family itself, but to internalize benevolence as a moral quality. If we follow Aristotle to leave the family in order to establish the *polis*, we must begin with a "unit of action" of the individual, a powerful conception with an enduring legacy. From individualized thought in Greek philosophy, to individualized faith in Protestantism, to individualized rights grounded in property in John Locke, the unit of action remains firmly grounded in the individual. This is what the status of belonging to the city, as citizens, essentially means. Rights-holding individuals in perpetual heroic struggle to defend these rights individually has been a dominant moral and aesthetic narrative. Systems theory suggests that the sizes of organizations are inherently limited by their levels of complexity; organizations would not come into being if they are too small, and would collapse under excessive complexity when they are too large. Aristotle suggests that a city should be neither too large nor too small. However, with the rise of industrialization and bureaucracy, economic organizations have become much larger than human organizations; we now seem to have a paradox in European cities. One of the greatest sociological anxieties in Europe and America, particularly since the age of industrialization and the traumatic experiences of the First World War, was that organizations have become "impersonal," leading to the decline of the rights-holding individual as the unit of action. Weber's penetrating diagnosis of the iron cage of bureaucracy is only eerily confirmed by today's data analytics and robotic technologies. This paradox is perhaps solved through the idea of federation of modular structures; while maintaining much larger economic organizations, the modular structures continue to maintain a "most effective size" of human organizations. The federated political unions of the United States and the European Union are grounded in this "dynamic equilibrium" between individual agency and maximum size of organization. Large architectural firms such as Gensler and AECOM tend to adopt a similar strategy of modular organization, necessitated by multiple locations demanded by globalization.

The "unit of action" in China is much larger. It is at least as large as the family, but is it often enlarged by "family-like" units such as village kinship groups, clan associations, a contemporary work unit (*danwei*), and a commercial company. Within these larger units of action, social bonding is often expressed through analogous familial relationships. Larger units of action are capable of forming larger organizations with simpler structures. China's "group action"—larger political and economic units of action based on simpler social structures—seems to be more sympathetic to larger economic organizations; this could indeed account for the incredibly fast and large-scale economic development in China.

Perhaps the most deep-rooted political ideal in China is the notion of the Great Sameness. First expounded in the Confucianist canon *Book of Rites* (*Liji*, 475 BCE–221 BCE), the political vision known as the Great Sameness under the Heaven (*tianxia datong*) has a powerful grip on China's political imagination, even though interpretations differ greatly. The founder of modern China, Sun Yat-sen, used it to advance his republican alternative to China's long tradition of imperial rule, arguing that republicanism was much closer to the political vision of Confucius than the imperial system. Xi Jinping's "Community of Shared Future for Mankind" contains the key characters "community of sameness" (*gongtongti*), reflecting, to some degree, the enduring value of the Confucianist political strategy. Known popularly as "harmonious society" (*hexie shehui*), this social management strategy believes that the decrease of individual autonomy is far outweighed by the benefits of greater care: imperfect as it is in China today, this political system attempts to provide a complete set of support infrastructure in cities. In many ways, Singapore already practices a version of this social infrastructure since the 1960s. The Confucianist political strategy is much closer to *realpolitik* instead of abstract ideals; it measures its political efficacy through material differences more than conceptual ones. The state provision of housing, medical care, education, and transportation in Singapore is fundamental to the well-being of its citizens and its largely peaceful multi-racial and multi-cultural society; with a history of social unrest and little natural resources, Singapore can indeed be seen as a functional example of Confucianist political strategy of the Great Sameness. With the precedent of Singapore in mind, this harmony model certainly has great potential in China.

Chinese cities are shaped by "group action" in two broad ways, first in how rural villages became urban areas in response to global manufacturing capacity, and second in how municipal governments invest in their future in relation to global knowledge economy. Chinese villages were impoverished in the 1960s and 1970s in the Mao era. However, a significant number of them did not believe collectivization was the problem of their economic failure; in fact, they continue to believe in Mao's wisdom in eradicating private land ownership. These villages maintained their collective landownership instead of privatization; they have formed much larger collective units and acted together in making agriculture larger in scale, and in developing village industries to take advantage of the world's demand in manufactured goods. They have in effect formed rural-urban village corporations to compete in the larger marketplace of goods and finance. Collective ownership and corporate group action, instead of being ideological oxymoron, complement each other to construct a prosperous life. Most villagers are incredulous at their success in creating a viable economy, turning their villages into small cities.

With immense pressure of expanding economic activities, many large cities in China were in a hurry to invent their own knowledge economies, seeing the extraordinary rise of Silicon Valley and the universities nestled in clusters of technological companies as their precedent. Their solution is the university city, a fast and municipally managed clustering of research and teaching facilities that would quickly bring a knowledge economy to their cities. In parallel, the university city also serves the important purpose of utilizing agricultural land for urban development. While the collectively owned "village-urban corporations" have been wildly successful, university cities are facing steeper challenges; perhaps the group action model is too simplistic to accommodate the sophistication of academia, which simply cannot be enlarged quickly as economic organizations. Universities, unlike village industries, are complex environments with much longer processes of metabolism; clustering is perhaps an incidental feature rather than a defining one.

Group action, with its capacity for larger sizes and simpler social structures, gives us a range of realities that compel us to reconsider Weber's characterization of the "Asiatic city" as lacking in "cityness." The political autonomy of the male citizens in the Greek *polis* and that of the merchant class in Weber's Protestant city were clearly constructed on the foundations of institutionalized inequality and discrimination; freedom and equality of peers are only possible through subjugation and exploitation in this model. China's cities of group action and group care, despite their rough edges, could produce a genuinely different and viable city never before seen since the Greek *polis* and the medieval monastery.

The Architectural Profession

The Chinese architectural profession seems to have found its form in embracing China's astonishing urbanization in the past four decades. In many ways, China's professional practice is both a product and a producer of the effects of cultural bottlenecks in the flow of money, people, goods, and materials. Dominating the scene of professional practice are large firms known as Design Institutes (*shejiyuan*) such as Shanghai Xiandai Architectural Design (SXDA), China Architecture Design & Research Group (CAG), Beijing Institute of Architectural Design (BIAD), Shenzhen General Institute of Architectural Design and Research (SADI), and the Architectural Design and Research Institute of Tongji University (TJAD). All of them evolved from their former status as state-managed institutions of architectural design, and now offer highly competitive all-in-one services in architecture, landscape, planning, and infrastructural services with high competence and reliability. The professionalization of architects is a European idea; unlike medieval Europe, artisans never formed independent and powerful guilds in China. On the other hand, state management of architecture has much deeper roots. In the Chinese cultural context, the politics of immanence, rather than that of transcendentality, has meant a close and material relationship between governance and architecture; instead of being symbols of power and sites of intellectual discourse, architecture in China was traditionally the very substance of power and status. China's imperial administration managed the design of buildings from Ministry of Rites (*Libu*) and the construction of buildings from Ministry of Works (*Gongbu*); they enforced a strict hierarchy of buildings through the size of timber (*cai*) and the number of intercolumniation (*jian*), underscoring the importance of governance through the materiality of architecture. Cultivated in the cultural environment of figuration, this political tradition has maintained its presence in architecture, even though the outward forms of material hierarchies have changed dramatically.

This long-standing relationship between the state and architecture lend tremendous legitimacy and trust to the Design Institutes as preferred consultants in large-scale projects; it shapes a distinctive condition of professional practice: Design Institutes at the center and private architectural practices at the margins. Smaller private practices have offered truly exciting ideas and buildings in recent decades by paralleling European and American practices, but it is the Design Institutes that are articulating the architectural profession for China. They are blazing new trails of "group design." The institutions of group design have become deeply integrated in the production of key features of Chinese cities. Unlike many foreign architectural design firms operating in China, they seem to hold the powerful cultural keys of ten thousand things, figuration, and group action that give us the urban realities of the typological drift of Chinese cities.

1
Max Weber, *The City*, New York: The
Free Press, 1958; *The Religion of China:
Confucianism and Daoism*, New York: The
Free Press, 1951, p.13.

2
Data from National Bureau of Statistics
of China (http://data.stats.gov.cn/)

3
Hsing You-tien, *The Great Urban
Transformation: Politics of Land and
Property in China*, Oxford: Oxford
University Press, 2010; Stephan
Haggard, *Developmental States*,
Cambridge: Cambridge University
Press, 2018.

4
Marcel Granet, *La Pensée Chinoise*
(Paris, La Renaissance du livre, 1934).

5
François Jullien, *Detour and Access,
Strategies of Meaning in China and
Greece*, New York: Zone Books, 2004.

6
Li Shiqiao, "Abundance," in
Understanding the Chinese City, London:
Sage Publications, 2014.

7
Craig Clunas, *Empire of Great Brightness:
Visual and Material Cultures in Ming
China, 1368–1644*, Honolulu: University
of Hawaii Press, 2007.

8
Mencius, *Teng Wen Gong*, third century
BCE, Part One.

9
Cheng, Hao and Cheng, Yi, *Collected
Works of the Two Chengs (Er Cheng Ji)*
(Beijing: Zhonghua Shuju, 1981), Yishu,
Chapter 11, p.123.

10
Ibid., *Yishu*, Chapter 4, p.73.

11
François Jullien, *The Propensity of
Things: Toward a History of Efficacy in
China*, New York: Zone Books, 1995.

12
Ferdinand de Saussure, *Course in
General Linguistics*, Chicago: Open
Court, 1972, p.14.

Drift
Trigger
One:

Ten Thousand Things

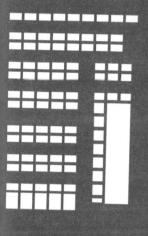

Ten Thousand Things

Yiwu, Xintang, and Gurao are three cities located in two of China's most dynamic regions, the Yangtze River Delta and the Pearl River Delta with a combined population of 260 million people. They represent a much larger set of cities in China functioning in similar ways: as distribution and wholesale centers, and as highly specialized production bases for a narrow range of goods such as cigarette lighters, socks, coffins, violins, underwear, jeans, etc. Together, these cities establish a vast network of production and distribution of continuously evolving commercial goods, however insignificant. Yiwu has since the 1980s set its ambition to be the marketplace of all goods in one place; in the process, it has undoubtedly created the most astonishing display of the profusion of goods to the greatest possible extent today. Xintang and Gurao combined factories with family workshops to form self-organizing systems of production of underwear and jeans, two of the most complex and labor intensive clothing items; Xintang and Gurao are not managed corporations, but highly specialized and highly flexible units of production that can shift gears with short notices. These cities are their endlessly specialized and flexible units; they are also their own rhizomic and complete supply chains. Exceedingly competitive in these ways, these cities have reinvented manufacturing of the Industrial Revolution, and brought the traditional notion of ten thousand things (*wanwu*) a stunning new reality never seen in history; the quantity and variety of goods are scaled for the entire world.

Globalization was perhaps never imagined to be in this form; what was known as the Washington Consensus—a neoliberalist global financial program created by the International Monetary Fund, the World Bank, and the United States Treasury demanding structural adjustments in return for investments—was centered on European and American economies. It seems to have been formulated on the basis of a modified colonial system, where periphery countries would offer higher profit margins through cheaper raw materials and labor, while center countries would instead invest in high value sectors of the global economy through an intensification of knowledge and innovation. China's establishment of "complete commodities systems" from production and distribution to research and innovation has disrupted the earlier assumptions of globalization. It has created an economic and social reality different enough to justify the talk of a Beijing Consensus as an alternative to the Washington Consensus. The notion of the Beijing Consensus is to recognize the emerging fact that Chinese cities may have begun with building a labor-intensive manufacturing sector, but they have shifted the center of globalization or at least created multiple centers, resulting in reverse flows in the knowledge economy. They illustrate the results of a typological drift. The very idea of economy in the Chinese intellectual context is constructed differently, as Michael Keith, Scott Lash, Jakob Arnoldi, and Tyler Rooker argue in their book *China Constructing Capitalism: Economic Life and Urban Change* (2013); economy, instead of conceived in contradistinction with society and politics, has been intertwined with society and politics as the lifeworld in China. The clustering of production, distribution, and research capacity, seen in the long civilizational history of China and its role in the Silk Roads, has always been central to its conception of "economic activities" as opposed to the Weberian "economic action." China's economic activities are integrated in the structure of social life. In this mode, and historically, the production and distribution of silk, tea, porcelain, and the accumulation of silver had in many ways structured the world economy. Andre Gunder Frank in *ReOrient:*

Global Economy in the Asian Age (1998) and Giovanni Arrighi in *Adam Smith in Beijing: Lineages of the 21st Century* (2007) have argued that China's economic decline in the nineteenth and twentieth centuries seems to be an exception in this long history.

Hard though it may be to look beyond the harsh realities of hurried productions of endless varieties of goods at the thinnest profit margins, Yiwu, Xintang, and Gurao have in them an embryonic form of future cities of abundance for China. Among the three cities, Yiwu is perhaps most ambitious to invent the next version of its economic activities. In their future developments, these cities are both about the profusion of goods and about the lifeworld intertwined with the profusion of goods. Profusion without guilt is a difficult moral territory in Indo-European cities; profusion, as in the baroque, is only possible as the excessive other to a well-proportioned quantity as the norm. Yiwu, Xintang, and Gurao come from an entirely different intellectual territory; they embrace the profusion of goods—and all the necessary material and human conditions to accomplish it—with a conviction and dedication not easily established in other cultures. Through the abundance of things, these cities are perhaps finding the richness of moral and aesthetic life described in one way in *The Plum in the Golden Vase* (*Jin Ping Mei*), the celebrated Ming novel detailing the delightful intersections of poetry, love, and silver with an openness hard to attain in our narrowly moralized age. It is in the richness of material life—the acceptance of all the material and sensual world has to offer to life—that the moral and aesthetic life can be brought to reality, much like the Ming merchants who transformed their silver-based wealth into the gardens of the *literati*, leaving us with a rich cultural resource deeply appreciated by all.

Zhejiang Province   Yiwu   International Trade City

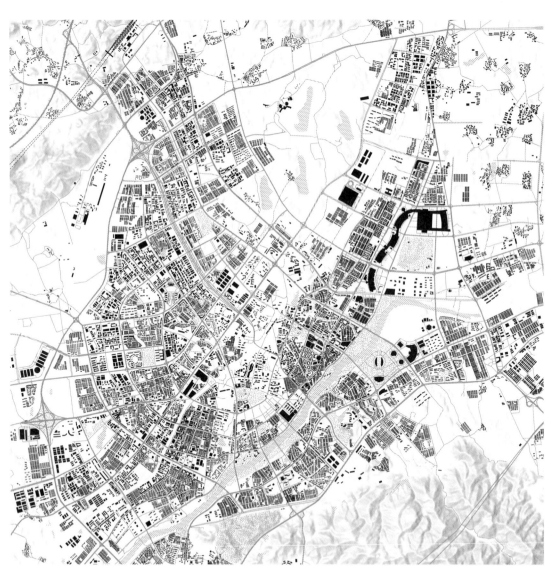

Yiwu, scale 1:100,000

Yiwu:
Postmodern Sublime

The store-lined interior corridors of Yiwu are more provoc-
ative than they first appear; at the first glance, they are
almost embarrassingly modest next to the aspiring gran-
deur of those of the Venetian in Macau and the determined
luxury of those of Central in Hong Kong. They have none
of the contrived totalities of meaning embedded in the
signifiers decorating the Mall of America and the Dubai
Mall. In Yiwu, the corridors offer a physical setting for
a normative encounter with commodities that suggest
affordability and choice; not semi-packaged lifestyle
choices but economic value at its barest essentials. Yiwu's
modesty radiates the attraction of bargains, which can be
intoxicating. However, very quickly, the excitement of this
first encounter turns into something that is difficult to
define: perhaps it is the inability to grasp the sheer number
and range of commodities, perhaps it is a lingering fear of
striking the worst deal out of all possible deals, perhaps it
is the total exhaustion resulting from the primal motiva-
tion for an overview of value, perhaps it is the frustration
with sameness in endless variety. It is something akin to
flipping through hundreds of television channels and surf-
ing over thousands of websites eventually finding nothing
to watch or buy. The extreme corridoral monotony provides the key to this experience; clearly no one teaches
Kevin Lynch in Yiwu. As one shifts from animate excitement to abject inaction as a consumer, Yiwu's corridors
take on a menacing character. Like in a science fiction
or horror movie, one is trapped in never-ending tunnels
of commodities; their welcoming smile now turns into a
malicious grin, engulfing your body and extracting your
energy and financial resources. All of a sudden, the hedo-
nistic utopia of value and choice turns into a Gibsonian
dystopia of entrapment.

Arranging stalls along a walkway is as universal
an instinct as making wheels; one does not have to go to
architectural or planning schools to learn how to do this.
Street markets, as they are found in almost all human
settlements throughout the world, perhaps have been the
most enduring feature of communities and cities. The
arcade gave Paris its character in the nineteenth century,
the Christmas market defines Vienna at times of festiv-
ity, the five-foot way makes Singapore and Kuala Lumpur

Figure 1: Merchandise Mart in Chicago,
1930, developed by Marshall Field &
Co., designed by Graham, Anderson,
Probst & White, photograph by Carol M.
Highsmith, Library of Congress, https://
www.loc.gov/item/2011630447/

Figure 2: AmericasMart in Atlanta, 1957, designed by John Portman, photograph by Aprose793, wikimedia commons

examples of the tropical city, and the Golden Computer Arcade puts Hong Kong on the map of affordable tech that inspired enduring classics such as *Blade Runner* and *Ghost in the Shell*. Shopping malls are ideals; they mimic the street but romanticize it at the cost of the city. Draining its urban energy into containers, shopping malls leave the city to die a slow death, replacing it with rows and rows of homogenous spaces for contented consumers living in relative and abject isolation. Walkways can be spiritually and socially elevated; the stoa of the agora, the passages of the forum, the colonnades of the Vatican, and the corridors of imperial Beijing make use of the potentials of linear walkways to advance political, social, and religious goals.

But the corridors in Yiwu are something else. Lining the corridors of the International Trade City are over 75,000 stalls with a total building area of 5.5 million square meters. These stalls sell 1.8 million distinctly different kinds of commodities in 26 broad categories. They employ 210,000 salespersons and attract 210,000 visitors per day. In 2017, the total transaction value at the Trade City reached 122.6 billion rmb, an over 31,000-fold increase from that of 1982 when the first phase of the Trade City was built, which stood at 3.9 million rmb. These commodities reach all corners of the world through direct export clearances from Yiwu, fanning out to the major land, sea, and air transportation hubs in China, then to other parts of the world. One recent development has been a dedicated rail called "Yiwu-Xinjiang-Europe" line—"a caravan with no need to feed on grass" as China's CCTV dubbed it with a clear reference to the much cherished history of the Silk Roads—that stretches 13,000 kilometers from Yiwu to Madrid over 21 days, passing through important locations of Kazakhstan, Russia, Belarus, Poland, Germany, and France. In 2015, 1,988 containers were transported from Yiwu to Europe, and 204 containers were transported from Europe to Yiwu. Yiwu, a *stallopolis*, has been designed and constructed at the very outset with this enormous network of exchange in mind—which is in itself a mind-bending reality as it is almost impossible to "imagine" this network of exchange as physical entities.

When Jean-François Lyotard wrote his *The Postmodern Condition: A Report on Knowledge* in 1979, he anticipated an ever shortening of contract cycles, which allows outsourcing to take place: outsourcing of not only knowhow but also emotions. This is a most recent material manifestation of the logic of capital, as David Harvey

argues, through a "spatial displacement"—an ability to
spread contractual arrangements across geography in
search of larger and larger profit margins by shedding
more and more moral responsibilities—that results in
globalization. Perhaps they did not quite anticipate the
scale and speed with which this has taken place today.
Yiwu, among countless other cities in China and throughout the world, has taken this spatial displacement in the
world-system to heart and for granted. Instead of under-
cutting the pricing of commodities through specialization
and efficiency, Yiwu chose to build the ultimate marketplace to gather all commodities under heaven. It plays a
central role in the distribution of commodities that are
produced in the surrounding Yangtze River Delta. This
makes perfect sense for Yiwu. When Lyotard was musing
over the shortening of contract cycles in 1979, Yiwu did not
have enough food to feed its population, let alone pondering over neoliberalist strategies of making a profit; in 2015,
Yiwu's GDP is 16.2 billion US dollars. Yiwu does not have
sufficient farmland for its population; during inter-crop
seasons, small farm peasants began to trade brown sugar
for chicken feathers to enrich the soil and increase the
productivity of the soil. Initially seen to be a "capitalist" enterprise, this practice finally received government
approval in the early 1980s; an explosion of trade took place
and it expanded to all kinds of small commodities. China's
Open Door Policy, and its eventual joining of the World
Trade Organization, gave Yiwu an extraordinary opportunity to play a role in the world economy. If the Opium War
was China's first entry into the fledgling world system in
the nineteenth century, the Open Door Policy was China's
second entry. This time, technologies, transportation,
multinational finance, and the development of consumer
society are dramatically new, resulting in Yiwu's determination to maintain its mono-function as a *non plus
ultra* of the commodities market compared to Chicago's
Merchandise Mart (figure 1) and Atlanta's AmericasMart
(figure 2)—an urban condition that descended from the lin-
eage of Liverpool and Detroit. Yiwu is both a consequence

When Lyotard was musing over the shortening of
contract cycles in 1979, Yiwu did not have enough
food to feed its population, let alone pondering over
neoliberalist strategies of making a profit.

and a creator of today's throwaway culture—a manifestation of Lyotard's shortening of contract cycles embodied in the life-spans of commodities—that is so fundamentally different from Liverpool and Detroit.

Fredric Jameson, in his classic essay "Postmodernism, the Cultural Logic of Late Capitalism" first published in 1984, speculated on a notion of "postmodern sublime." Jameson noted a reduction of depths in the arts; from Van Gogh's peasant shoes to Warhol's diamond dust shoes, from Munch's scream figure to Warhol's Monroe, there has been a profound shift from depth of meaning and alienation of subjectivity to surface effects and physical/emotional burnout. This movement captures Lyotard's observation of shortening of contract cycles, Harvey's argument of spatial displacement, and Sennett's narrative of the decline of "careers" in *curricula vitae* and the rise of "job experiences." If the sublime of the machine age gave us Futurism and Le Corbusier, what would be a postmodern sublime of intensities? Is it William Gibson's *Neuromancer*, Ridley Scott's *Blade Runner* (figure 3), or the Wachowskis' *Matrix* (figure 4)? Is it the feedback loop of data and matter in the form of parametric design and 3D printing? Is it the tectonic abandonment of warped planes and twisted volumes? All of them are too fictitious or symbolic to give us a sense of the twenty-first century sublime that can rival the great imageries of modernity—the smoke chimneys, the steam locomotives, the automobiles, and the airplanes. The physical presence of our machines that enable spatial displacement is a flat screen, deliberately mute in its tectonic manifestations through a series of "reduction" of visible features in the design of computers and mobile devices. The symbolic feedback loops, the warping planes and twisting volumes in architecture fail, by a large margin, to capture the immense, powerful, and menacing nature of the world-system in its enormous and ever moving systems of goods, people, money, and commodities. Instead of the analogue approximations of feedback loops in parametric design masquerading as sublime, the sheer presence of throwaway commodities is perhaps a much more effective measure of the immensity of the system in its complexity, its impulses in material forms, and its pathologies in commodities abuse. Yiwu's corridors are not comparable to a Hadid fluidity, a Gehry composition, or a SOM slickness; they are very much unlike a themed development, a *xiaoqu* or a *danwei*. Yiwu's corridors have no aesthetic pretension and no political ideology. Yiwu's

Figure 3: *Blade Runner*, directed by Ridley Scott, The Ladd Company Shaw Brothers Blade Runner Partnership / Warner Brothers, 1982

corridors do not simulate meaningful and pleasurable human experiences: subjectivity, creativity, aesthetic pleasure, love, care, community, and society are faint conceptions receiving little mention in Yiwu.

Figure 4: *Matrix Reloaded*, directed by the Wachowskis, Village Roadshow Pictures Silver Pictures NPV Entertainment / Warner Brothers, 2003

Yiwu's corridors, in their ability to simultaneously excite emotions and thwart the urge to make sense, stand a chance to be an object of postmodern sublime in the world-system. Designed by the throwaway culture of today and enabled by the impatient multinational capital, Yiwu's corridors redefine human life within them (children doing homework in their commodity-filled glass boxes and playing hide and seek underneath escalators) and in distant places (locations of consumption with excess and abandonment) in their own image of ungraspable immensity and banality. Yiwu's corridors create the bonds between data centers, manufacturing bases, transportation systems, and shopping malls as the great intermediate and expansive gray zone, where tenuous and absurd usefulness are exchanged and tedious logistics of movement are actualized, where no meaningful ornamentation and dramatization can be found, where relentless drive for efficiency and profit of the world-system at the expense of the environment is the most manifest. We don't know, when globalization finishes its energetic and reckless expansion, how the corridors of Yiwu can be preserved as a tantalizing future "postmodern heritage" in architecture.

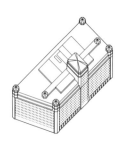

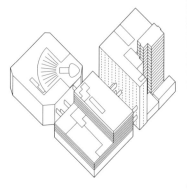

High Point Market
High Point, North Carolina
1909

The Merchandise Mart
Chicago, Illinois
1930

AmericasMart Atlanta
Atlanta, Georgia
1957

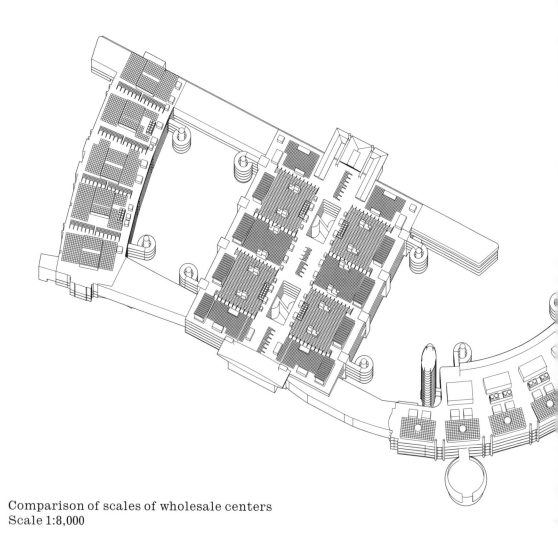

Comparison of scales of wholesale centers
Scale 1:8,000

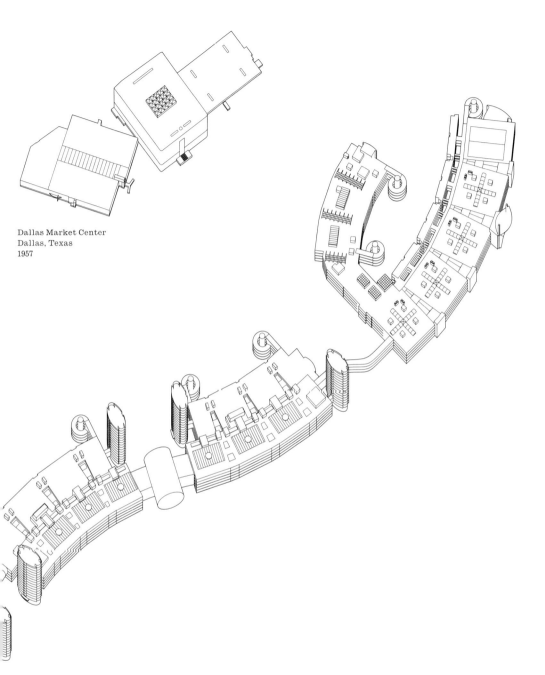

Dallas Market Center
Dallas, Texas
1957

International Trade City
Yiwu, Zhejiang Province
2002–2011

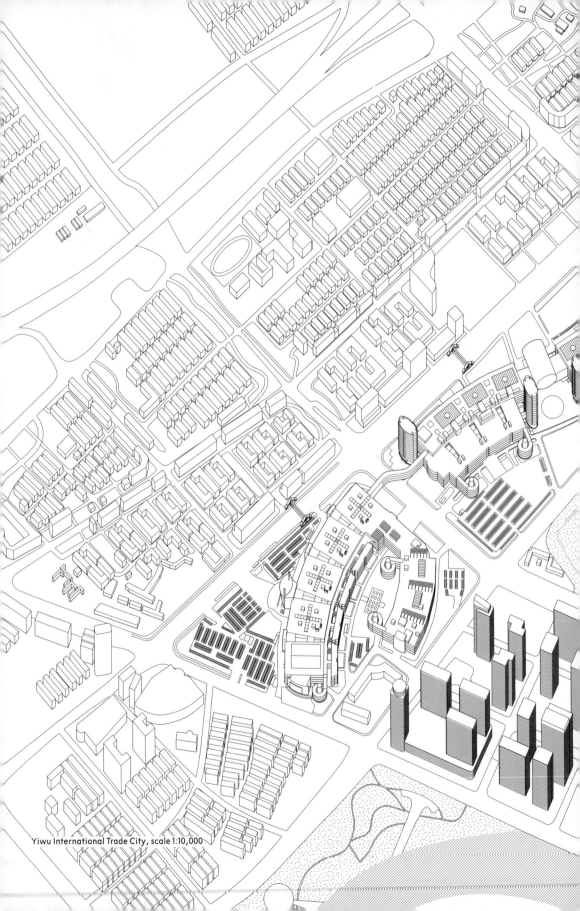

Yiwu International Trade City, scale 1:10,000

The Logic of Logistics

Connected with the transportation networks in China and the world, the International Trade City is dominated by the logic of the movement of goods in and out of it. The city's roads extend into the building three dimensionally in the form of spiraled ramps and take over most of the elevations to create a seamless network of vehicular access. At the end of this network of vehicular access are long loading docks allowing store managers to receive and send off commodities, which become the interface to the inner transportation network that is accessed on foot with carts.

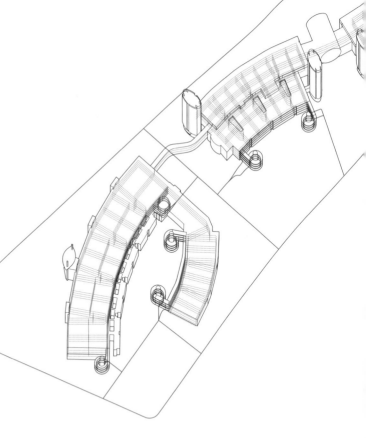

———— cars and trucks
·············· carts and bikes

International Trade City
Circulation
Scale 1:10,000

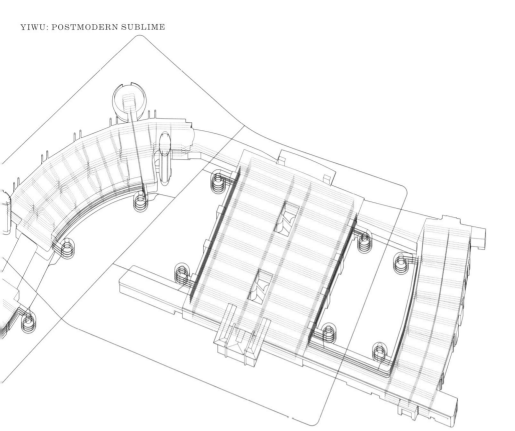

A ramp access to the loading docks and parking lots on every level

Atria

The vast interior of the International Trade City is organized along a series of multi-level voids facilitating orientation through the visual connection between the commodities on different floors as well as vertical pedestrian movement. These atria also provide daylight, resting stations with massage chairs, coffee shops, and fruit stands.

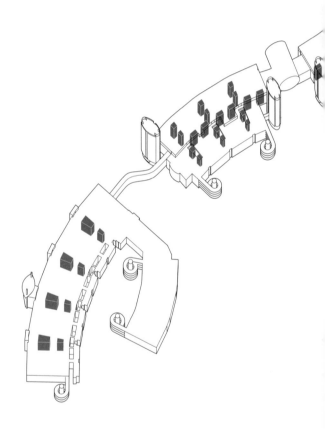

International Trade City
Atria
Scale 1:10,000

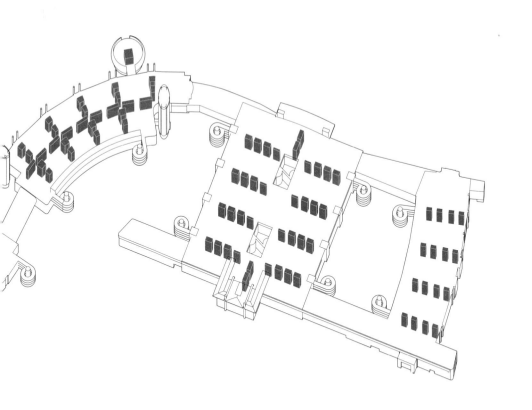

The main entrance lobby in District 4

District 1

District 2

District 3

Pedestrian Network

The pedestrian network in each district is organized with a hierarchy of main thoroughfares and narrower alleyways, converging to the atria and entrance spaces, vertical circulation hubs and loading docks.

Shopowners waiting for customers along the edge of the atrium with their shop still in view

A wider passageway leading to an atrium provides a quiet resting place for a shopowner and her baby

District 4

District 5

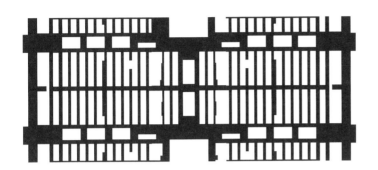

Pedestrian network module per district
Scale 1:4,000

A main pedestrian thoroughfare in District 1

A narrow alleyway

Showrooms

The showrooms are based on modular units that are combined or subdivided based on their locations, the type, and size of commodities, and the rental cost.

A standard-sized showroom maximizing display surfaces

A standard showroom subdivided into two showrooms in the jewelry section of District 1

The World Market for Small Commodities

The five phases (districts) of the International Trade City trace
the progression of Yiwu from a regional to a national to a
global trading hub. They also embody a gradual increase in
quantity, quality, and variety of goods flowing through Yiwu.
Districts are comprised of four to five levels with a total floor
area of 5.5 million square meters. Showrooms of similar commodities are grouped according to types of goods forming
specialized clusters on each floor.

International Trade City, District 4

District 1

4F Factory Outlets
3F Ornament Accessories
    Porcelain and Crystal
    Components for Accessories
    Picture Frames
    Tourism Craft
    Decorative Handicrafts
    Festive Handycrafts
2F Jewelry and Accessories
    Hair Ornaments
1F Common Toys
    Electric Toys
    Inflatable Toys
    Plush Toys
    Artificial Flowers
    Artificial Flowers Accessories

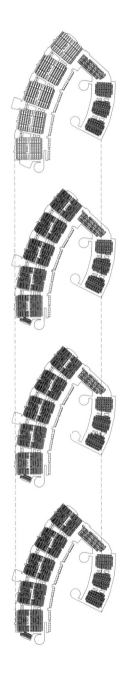

District 1
Scale 1:15,000

District 2

5F   Factory Outlet
      Foreign Trade
      Multifunctional Hall
      Roof Parking
4F   Electronics
      Cameras
      Batteries
      Lamps
      Flashlights
      Bags and Suitcases
3F   Clocks and Watches
      Small Home Appliances
      Kitchen and
      Bathroom Hardware
      Telecommunication
2F   Hardware and Tools
      Electronic Products
      Locks
1F   Suitcases and Bags
      Rainwear
      Umbrellas

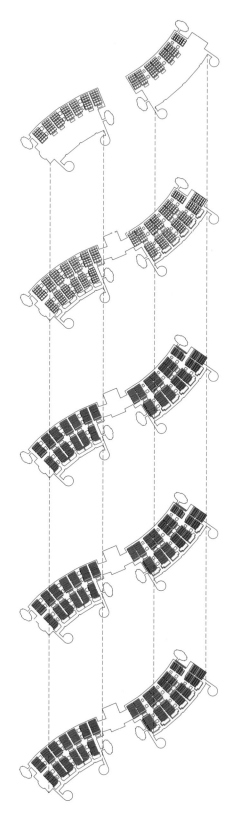

District 2
Scale 1:15,000

District 3

5F   Painting
       Roof Parking
4F   Factory Outlets
3F   Sports and Leisure Supplies
       Zippers
       Buttons
       Accessories
       Mirrors and Combs
       Cosmetics
2F   Sports Equipment
       Sports and Leisure Supplies
       Sporting Articles
       Office Supplies and
       Stationery
1F   Pens and Ink
       Paper Articles
       Glasses

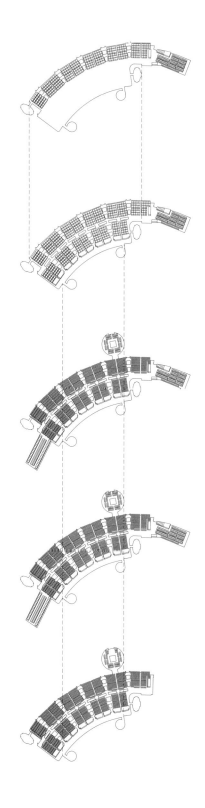

District 3
Scale 1:15,000

District 4

5F Factory Outlets
    Tourist Shopping Center
    Printed Pictures
4F Belts
    Scarves
    Bras and Underwear
3F Shoes
    Threads and Strings
    Lace
    Neckties
    Woolen Yarns
    Towels
2F Daily Consumables
    Knitted and Cotton Products
    Gloves and Mittens
    Hats
1F Socks
    Parking

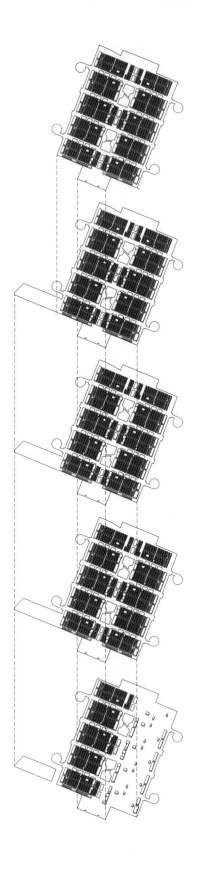

District 4
Scale 1:15,000

District 5

5F E-Commerce Service Zone
4F Automobile Accessories
    Car and Motorcycle Parts
    Pet Products
3F Curtain Fabrics
    Knitted Textiles
    Raw Materials for Knitting
    Wedding Supplies
2F Bedding
    Wedding Supplies
    Hair Products
    DIY Handicrafts
1F Sales Exhibition Center for
    African and ASEAN Products
    Other Imports
    Food and Health Food
    Jewelry and Handicrafts
    Clothing, Hats, and Shoes
    Articles of Daily Use

District 5
Scale 1:15,000

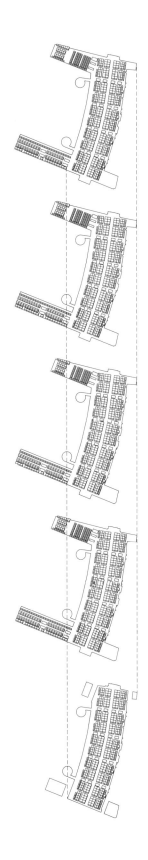

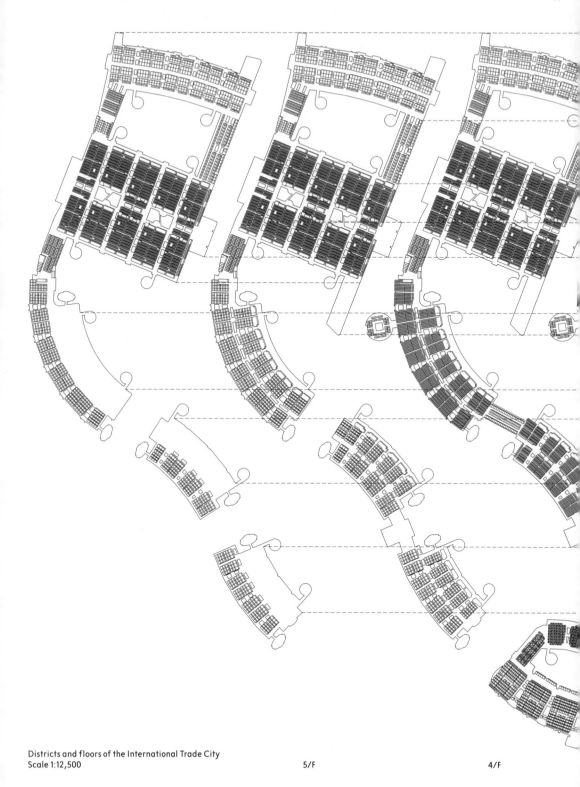

Districts and floors of the International Trade City
Scale 1:12,500

5/F

4/F

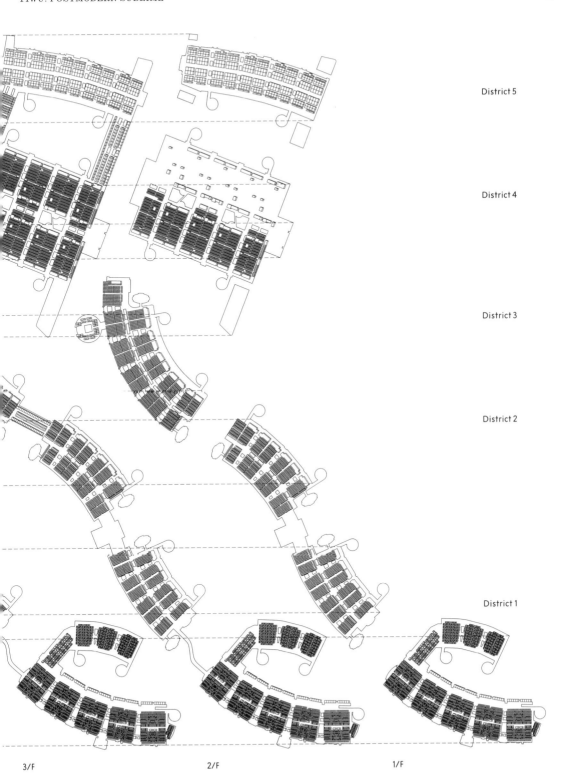

District 5

District 4

District 3

District 2

District 1

3/F   2/F   1/F

Social Life Reinventing the International Trade City

Designed with maximum functionality in mind, the
International Trade City accomodates a large and complex
population with diverse age and cultural backgrounds.
The daily lives of its users are transforming the strictly pragmatic spaces in inventive and surprising ways, bringing
a rich urban texture and liveliness to the otherwise cold interior. Historically the marketplace is never separated from
social life. Yiwu's determined pursuit of economic efficiency
in the context of globalization is met with cultural practices
adamantly reclaiming their presence.

The atria form the nexus of social life in the International
Trade City.

1

2

3

4

1   Many of the stalls in the International Trade City are run by family businesses. While the men usually take care of the factory, the women enter the double-role of shop keeper and mother, attending to both the customers and their children.
2   Small children below school age spend all day in the Trade City. Mothers appreciate the clean, air-conditioned, and safe environment, as well as the proximity to their young children during their work. The atria in particular are appreciated for their spaciousness and daylight, offering space for gathering, toy rides, and running on the ground or up and down the stairs and escalators.
3–5   Older children are here on the weekends. On weekdays they arrive after school and spend their time working on their homework or playing until the closing of business hours.

5

1

2

3

4

1   Restaurants—in relatively small numbers—are located on
the periphery of the ground floors as well as lining the interface
between the parking garage and the trade city—internal space is
too valuable to be given to food provision.
2   Around lunch time, mobile food carts deliver warm meals
into the spaces of the Trade City. The styrofoam boxes keep the
food warm and may also serve as a provisional eating counter.
3   A table and red plastic chairs turn the corridor into a
make-shift family dining room.
4–5   Fruit basket carriers and small fruit stalls provide snacks
throughout business hours.

5

6

7

6   Traders from Africa and the Middle East exchange banter
with the Chinese showroom owner after a successful transaction.
7   Middle-Eastern traders prepare for prayer in one of the
atrium spaces.
8   The alleyway transforms into a place of rest and play.
9   An elderly woman and her granddaughter watch a group of
women sorting and re-packaging goods in the jewelry section of
District 1.

8

9

Atria, showrooms, and social life in the
International Trade City, District 1, scale 1:200

Guangdong Province   Guangzhou   Xintangzhen

Xintang, scale 1:100,000

Xintang:
Stitching the Global Casual

Nothing seems to capture the idea of a global homogenous culture better than the denim fabric; Xintang rose rapidly in the 1990s to bring a new level of accessibility—through low cost, high volume, speed of delivery, and sheer variety—for the insatiable global desire for denim clothing. Xintang is part of a district of Guangzhou called Zengcheng with an area of 85 square kilometers and a population of about 600,000 consisting of 32 villages. About 360,000 are migrant workers. It is the location of about 4,700 enterprises, among them 60 percent, or about 3,000, are related to denim products, with a capacity of producing 2.5 million pieces of denim clothing per day. Xintang is equipped to function in the entire process of making denim clothing: from spinning, dyeing, weaving, printing, manufacturing, to the many washing cycles. Sixty percent of China's denim products and 30 precent of denim exports come from Xintang.[1] At its peak in early 2010s, Xintang supplied about 40 percent of the jeans in the United States.[2]

Figure 1: Gold miners talking, photograph by Russell Lee, Mogollon, New Mexico, 1940. Library of Congress, https://www.loc.gov/item/2017742525/.

Denim gained its defining character from the indigo dye originating from India, and from the weaving and tailoring in Nimes (denim, *Serge de Nîmes*) and Genoa (jeans). In the eighteenth century, the cloth maker Levi Strauss, a Bavarian immigrant to America, supplied the gold excavators in San Francisco with strong work clothes by using the denim fabric made of thick cotton twill weaving (the weft goes under two or more warp strings), reinforced with metallic bolts, and branded with leather labels. Cotton was plentiful, thus the extra weight of the fabric made economic sense as work clothes. These demanding functional considerations defined the feature of denim clothing (figure 1). From the 1930s onwards, Hollywood made cowboy movies with their protagonists wearing jeans (not historically accurate but facts never got in the way of storytelling). More importantly, movies in the 1950s portrayed rebellious characters, performed by Marlon Brando in *The Wild One* (figure 2), James Dean in *Rebel Without a Cause* (figure 3), and Marilyn Monroe in *The Misfits* (figure 4), all wearing jeans.[3] Jeans were the alternative that signified a spirit to break with conventions, a postwar sentiment that emerged with relative peace and prosperity in America. These portrayals in popular entertainment unleashed a desire of the baby boomers for denim clothing.

Figure 2: Marlon Brando in *The Wild One*, Stanley Kramer Productions / Columbia Pictures, 1953

Figure 3: James Dean in *Rebel Without a Cause*, Warner Brothers, 1955

Jeans have never left the cinema since then, and these movies helped transform jeans from uncomfortable tough work clothes to perhaps the most popular clothing style of the world today: there is almost no class, race, age, culture, gender, occasion where jeans (and denim clothing) are not appropriate. From rebelliousness to conformity, jeans have been able to change and adapt to transcend the baby boomer generation in a way few other fashion trends have been able to.

As a global material, denim played a key role in the casualization of the world. It is, in many ways, an inevitable development; over the past one hundred years, social stratification has removed its symbolic visual signification prominently displayed through dress codes, which served as a material parallel to manners.[4] The twentieth-century society has been a great equalizing society with the rise of consumerism; possession of commodities mimics the possession of social status to generate an ingenious system of consumption as social relations. Denim has become a potent symbol of equalization paralleling that in power and desire. Denim has a working class origin but is culturally elevated through decades of association with the rebellious spirit. The naturalness of cotton, the endurance of the twill weave, the blur of dye over time, have privileged denim as the embodiment of the global casual.

Like so many other Chinese cities that invest in the production of global commodities, Xintang made denim clothing available and affordable by being efficient, adaptable, and tolerant of an enormously polluting process of production. While the casual and worn out look of denim may be intrinsic to the work of San Francisco gold diggers, it is today the result of a highly labor-intensive process: the whiskers pattern, the distress effect, the highlighting areas are created individually with stone rubbing, spraying, and chemical washing, sometimes mixed with pumice stone. A single pair of jeans embodies about 2,000 gallons of

The naturalness of cotton, the endurance of the twill weave, the blur of dye over time, have privileged denim as the embodiment of the global casual.

water (depending on the level of casualness in the washed effects), much of it is discharged as contaminated water without much treatment.[5] The traditional indigo blue is achieved with dye derived from plants (*indigofera tinctoria*); synthetic dye was introduced in 1897 and combined with sulphur dye in the 1980s to acquire new effects, and to add new colors such as black, olive, and burgundy.[6] Xintang's willingness to overlook environmental pollution, until around 2018, made it competitive as a production base for denim clothing. Xintang is located next to the Dongjiang River with good access to water; it is dominated by the central Guangzhou-Shenzhen Boulevard, with many of the old villages located to the south of the boulevard, surrounded by factories. Like in Gurao, Xintang offers a combination of family workshops and large-scale production facilities, which are highly intertwined. A family workshop can punctuate large amounts of pockets ready for leather labels, which are branded in a second family workshop with a few leather press machines, fixed with bolts in a third family workshop, before returning them to a large scale manufacturer of jeans. This family based specialization—down to the rolling of fabric in the workshop operated by a single person with a single fabric-rolling machine—employs a large amount of low cost labor without accumulating hiring risks for manufacturers. This distribution of risks creates endless flexibility and fast adjustment to new orders and market conditions.

Figure 4: Marilyn Monroe with Clark Gable in *The Misfits*, Seven Arts Productions / United Artists, 1961

Along the main Guangzhou-Shenzhen Boulevard is the Xintang (International) Jeans City with more than 3,000 shops, the centerpiece of Xintang that displays finished products, surrounded by suppliers of semi-finished materials such as denim fabrics. Xintang has over 1,000 registered brands of denim clothing, all of them are in a highly competitive market. The Jeans City is planned as a series of rectangular blocks of commercial spaces forming a large square, where its annual International Festival of Cowboy Culture is held. The use of aluminum cladding and large areas of greenish reflective glass is within the norm of aspiring modernity in small Chinese cities, but the scale of uniformity produces an impressive environment. The humid sub-tropical southern Chinese town with neither the culture of horsemanship nor a pastoral economy cannot be further removed from the cowboy culture of American West, but globalization has created a Chinese city as a drift of type: an abrupt grafting of a distant culture only made sense through the logic of economy of production.

The production of the global casual—materialized through denim—seems to have established its place in the world; market research suggests that the denim sector maintains an average growth rate of 3–5 percent in the next decade. With higher wages and the stricter environmental laws already put in place in Xintang, which forced many of its dyeing facilities to relocate to inner provinces of China, it is far from certain that Xintang will maintain its competitive edge and its position as the world's "capital of jeans". However, Xintang owes its existence to the production of the global casual: a profound transformation of a rebel cultural icon into a material of equalization in the global context.

1
Zengcheng government website:
http://www.zc.gov.cn/
2
Greenpeace report: http://
www.greenpeace.org/eastasia/
news/stories/toxics/2010/textile-
pollution-xintang-gurao/
3
S. G. Annapoorani, "Introduction
to Denim," in S. S. Muthu ed.,
Sustainability in Denim, Duxford:
Elsevier, 2017, pp.1–26. Jennifer Wright,
"The Complete History of Blue Jeans,"
https://www.racked.com/2015/2/27/8116465/
the-complete-history-of-blue-jeans-
from-miners-to-marilyn-monroe
4
For a discussion on manners and estate
in relation to social status, see Thorsten
Veblen, *The Theory of the Leisure Class*,
New York: Macmillan, 1899.
5
Stephen Leahy, *Your Water Footprint*,
New York: Firefly Books, 2014.
6
K. Amutha, "The Environmental
Impacts of Denim," in S. S. Muthu ed.,
Sustainability in Denim, p.38.

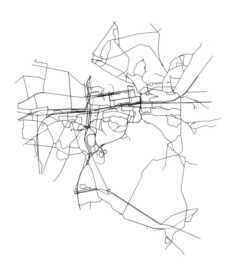

Wolfsburg: Volkswagen Cars
123,144 inhabitants (2012)
1 assembly plant
815,000 cars produced in 2015
0.9% of global production

Toyota City: Toyota Cars
426,126 inhabitants (2019)
3 assembly plants
762,000 cars produced in 2011
0.95% of global production

Detroit: General Motors, Ford, and Crysler Cars
672,681 inhabitants (2018)
2 assembly plants
1.7 million cars produced in 2017
1.75% of global production

Automobile production cities (high-cost technology-intensive products)
Scale 1:300,000

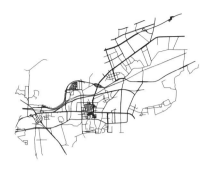

Xintang: Jeans
257,894 residents (2017) and 362,500 migrants
4,766 factories and manufacturing workshops (2016)
1 billion denim clothes produced annually (2013)
2.5 million denim clothes produced per day
30–40% of global blue jean production

Gurao: Underwear
184,755 residents (2017) and 120,000–220,000 migrants
1,080 factories and 2,800 family workshops
350 million bras and 430 million vests and underpants
produced annually (2016)
16% of global underwear production

Shaogang: Measuring Tape
61,559 residents (2017) and 30,000 migrants
4,800 factories
1.5 billion measuring tapes produced annually
80% of global production

Datang: Socks
76,000 residents (2020) and 100,000 migrants
3,143 factories (2015)
5 billion socks produced in 2018, 25.8 billion pairs of
socks produced in peak year 2014
35% of global production

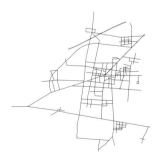

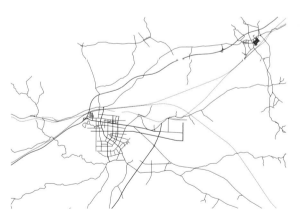

Zuangzhai: Coffins
85,684 residents (2017) and 27,000 migrants
2,569 factories and 5,000 workshops
740,000 coffins produced annually
60% of Japan's coffin production

Shaodong: Cigarette Lighter
184,755 residents (2017) and 140,000 migrants (2011)
112 factories
5 billion cigarette lighters produced annually
70% of global cigarette lighter production

Everyday item production cities (low-cost labor-intensive products)
Scale 1:300,000

Xintang International Jeans City, scale 1:2,500

1   Gate to the International Jeans City
2   A logistics center
3   A jeans business advertisement
4   A business center
5   A shop for chemical dyes
6   Second-hand machines for stonewashing jeans for sale,
after washing workshops moved to other parts of China due to
Xintang's water pollution control policies
7   Denim fabric used as motorbike cover
8   Migrant workers housing
9   The interior of a shop in the International Jeans City

5

6

7

8

9

1 A jeans sewing workshop
2 A fabric rolling workshop
3 A workshop specializing in making small cuts in
semi-processed denim fabric
4 Jeans on display in a small shop
5 A workshop specializing in stamping leather labels

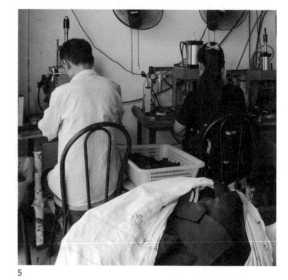

6

7

8

6–7   Schoolchildren fixing metal tags onto leather labels during
summer school recess
8   A worker cutting faux leather for the production of labels
9   A family workshop specializing in rivets and eyelets

9

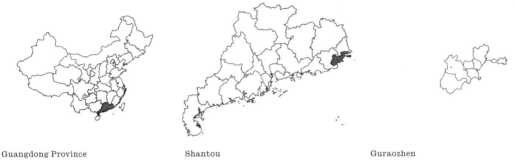

Guangdong Province

Shantou

Guraozhen

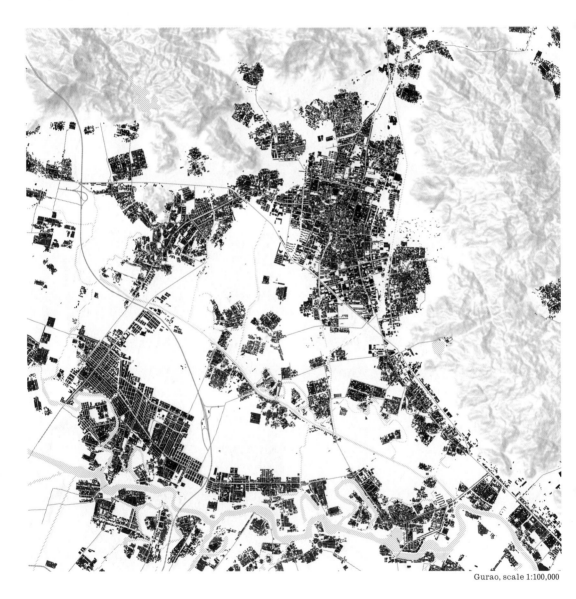

Gurao, scale 1:100,000

Gurao:
The Underworld of Underwear

Gurao's appearance is deceiving. Although a "town" (*zhen*) in the nomenclature of China's city classification, Gurao is in reality a small city with a population of around 184,700 (2017). It is located within the Chaoyang District of the City of Shantou, one of the first "treaty port" cities of China. Treaty port cities were created as the result of several treaties China signed with European powers in the late nineteenth century following the Opium War; the goal was to open these cities to European settlement and trade with enormous privileges of land and taxes. Shantou became a treaty port in 1858 as part of the Anglo-Chinese Treaty of Tientsin. This accounts for Gurao's strong connection with the overseas Chinese diaspora—it has more than 100,000 emigrants—in Asia and Southeast Asia, who changed Gurao's economic fortune from late twentieth century onwards.

Gurao, however, has an ancient history before European powers descended on its neighboring Shantou. Chaoyang County was established 1391 by the first Ming Emperor Hongwu, who focused his rule on the restoration of China's peasant cultural and land system, following a century of Mongol rule (Yuan dynasty 1279–1368) that weakened the idea of a peasant empire. Gurao proudly celebrates today Wen Tianxiang (1236–1283), a brilliant scholar and military general who fought bravely against the invading Mongol armies of Kublai Khan. In the summer of 1278, Wen retreated to Chaoyang County after a series of setbacks, and was captured by the Mongol army in the same year. Kublai Khan met Wen personally in 1283, offering him the last chance to serve the Yuan dynasty or face execution; Wen chose to die. For over 700 years, Gurao has commemorated Wen Tianxiang and the Chinese soldiers who gave up their lives in Gurao in their resistance to the Mongol invasion.

This proud history parallels a proud local culture, the Chaoshan culture. Just about every aspect of life—literature, poetry, clothes, food, architecture—are distinctive when compared with those in other parts of China. The traditional residential architectural form is basically courtyard based (figure 1), but the rooms are relatively narrow, and the courtyard formations are very regularly arranged into clear square or rectangular clusters with

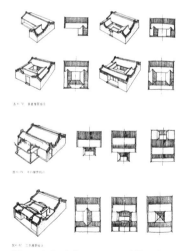

Figure 1: Basic house types of Chaoshan vernacular, courtesy of Lu Qi, *The Vernacular Architecture of Guangdong*, 2008, p. 138

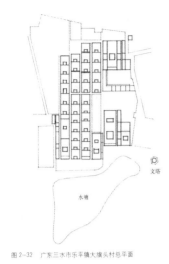

图 2-32　广东三水市乐平镇大旗头村总平面

Figure 2: Village layout of Chaoshan
vernacular, courtesy of Lu Qi, *The
Vernacular Architecture of Guangdong*,
2008, p.40

no centralities or village squares (figure 2). This strong,
family based regularity seems to suggest a connected
and conformist sensibility, one that could have helped its
transformation in the 1980s when Gurao gained a surprisingly different reputation in the world.

The first garment factory opened in Gurao in the
early 1980s, when Deng Xiaoping's China allowed private
enterprises to be established. Overseas Chinese investment
in underwear manufacturing flooded into Gurao; the most
rapid growth of Gurao's underwear production came in
the first decade of the twenty-first century, when China
joined the World Trade Organization in 2001. Despite its
ancient history, Gurao is known today in popular media
throughout the world as the "town of underwear." Gurao's
industrial output in 2017 was 37 billion rmb; 80 percent of
this output was underwear—around 350 million bras and
430 million vests and underpants annually—for China and
the rest of the world.[1] Gurao and other towns in China
made 2.9 billion bras in 2014, 60 percent of the world's total
according to the American business-consulting firm Frost
& Sullivan. It was ranked among National Comprehensive
1,000 Strong Towns in China in 2017, a ranking published
by China Society of Urban Economy.

There are more than 3,000 production facilities—
forming an ecology of underwear production with 1,080
enterprises and 2,800 family workshops—that are very
much evenly spread out in the city, giving the city an
appearance of undefined homogeneity. Underwear production is labor-intensive; this is why Gurao took it up
in the first place, aided by migration of rural labor. The
economist Michael Porter used "clusters" to describe the
logic of mass production; similar and related industries
group in one location to offer the most efficient production environment. However, China's production towns are
results of unique combinations of economic and cultural
features. The conformist Confucianist culture, very strong
in Gurao, reformulated the production cluster of underwear; family workshops, in this context, have made Gurao
incredibly versatile. A pupil's summer job to cut ribbons
into small pieces can be performed in a street shop (selling
accessories of underwear), while computerized embroi-
dery facilities can produce large quantities of ornamented
ribbons with speed and consistency. It is through this infrastructure of family workshops that the manufacturers
in Gurao maintain their competitiveness and flexibility.
Larger companies invest in high-tech equipment to make

seamless underwear with varying rigidity, the endless varieties of lace, elastic waistbands, push up bra foam molds, and metal ornaments can make economic sense when tiny processes of cutting, folding, pressing, and fixing them can be done in these family workshops in bulk with reasonable quality, high speed, and low cost. Anyone can walk into the city and, with the help of an experienced agent, can initiate a production of underwear—often clients bring their own samples when they arrive—at a price, quality, and speed not matched anywhere in the world. Gurao has more than 2,000 registered brands of underwear.

As a city Gurao seems to be what it is: a spread of small factories and family workshops with market streets—Gugui Road and Guguan Road—crossing the city. The pursuit of low cost has come so far with an enormous cost to the environment, with its water systems filled with pollution and waste from the dyeing and assembling. In 2018, a team of central government inspectors visited the city and found that the oxygen level in the river Heyong was 0.05 mg/L (1–6 mg/L are needed for bottom feeders and 4–5 mg/L are needed for shallow water fish), and that Shantou should have invested far greater resources (158 million rather than 6 million rmb) in its waste management.[2] Globalization thrives on negative externalities; Gurao is a textbook example of negative externality. The profit margin of the global business of the production of homogenized human sexuality through clothing is ironically located in an environmental degradation that is furthest removed from any notion of sensuality.

With each factory workshop enclosed in walls with gates, Gurao's perceivable outward appearance is dominated by information display, as if the entire city becomes a gigantic message board, in language and in things. The first kind of message boards, and not so unique to Gurao, are the ubiquitous displays of lunches and dinners as well as all commodities. The second kind of message boards are the large billboards of female figures in underwear, often branded with exotic sounding Chinese characters that

The profit margin of the global business of the production of homogenized human sexuality through clothing is ironically located in an environmental degradation that is furthest removed from any notion of sensuality.

make little sense in the Chinese language; bras and the production of in-your-face sexuality, it would seem, are still framed as foreign and exotic in this town. They dominate the cityscape. It seems surprising that Gurao does not have a central market for its underwear; they are all channeled individually through sales networks not visible in the city. Perhaps the lack of a central marketplace for underwear induces each manufacturer to display its own brand and product. In this sense, the third kind of message boards are in fact the endless shop windows packed with an astonishing amount of underwear components with endless variety. Quantity and variety of components clearly matter more than the idea of an aesthetic unit found in the art of window displays; in Gurao, as in many other Chinese cities, there is a pragmatic urgency to display the entirety of goods all in one place. The fourth kind of message boards are perhaps the most fascinating and most unique to Gurao: lists of job vacancies with details of types of jobs to be performed, benefits, and salaries.

Hardly a result of any urban planning and design, Gurao is nevertheless a city of globalization. Compared with the strongly figurated city centers and residential communities in other parts of China, Gurao is illustrative of the unremarkable mass of urbanization in their endless jostle for a place in the global economy.

1
https://www.economist.com/news/
china/21697004-one-product-towns-
fuelled-chinas-export-boom-many-
are-now-trouble-bleak-times-bra-town
2
http://www.xinhuanet.com/politics/
2018-06/21/c_1123013005.htm

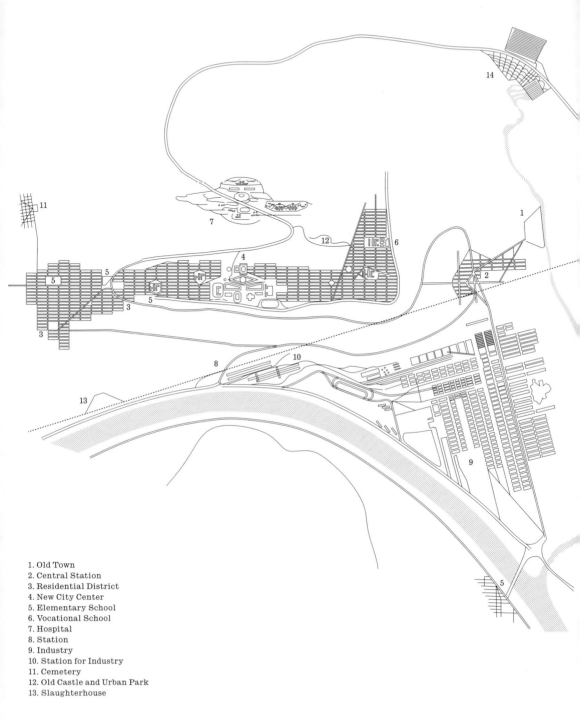

1. Old Town
2. Central Station
3. Residential District
4. New City Center
5. Elementary School
6. Vocational School
7. Hospital
8. Station
9. Industry
10. Station for Industry
11. Cemetery
12. Old Castle and Urban Park
13. Slaughterhouse

Cité Industrielle by Tony Garnier, scale 1:60,000

The ideal of functional zoning versus the practice of
mixing production and life

1. Single Factory Buildings
and Linear Shops
2. Village Houses and
Family Workshops
3. Factory Complexes and
Village Houses

Gurao, Guangdong, sca1e 1:20,000

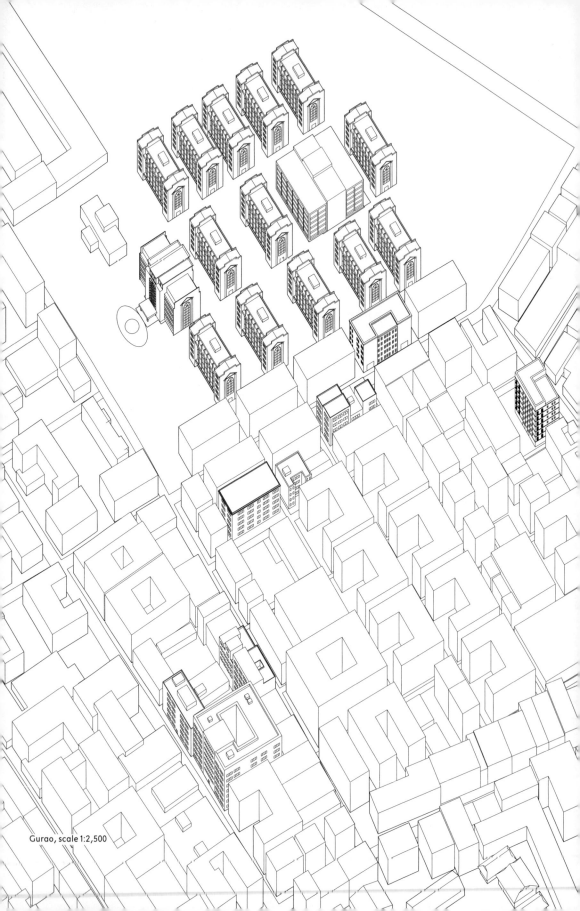

Gurao, scale 1:2,500

1

2

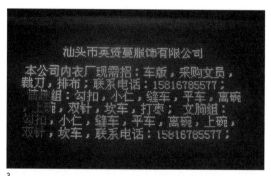

3

4

5

1   Gurao, view toward south onto single factory buildings and linear shops
2   A shop selling bra straps in bulk
3   LED display advertising specialist vacancies in an under-wear factory
4   A school girl cutting fabric tapes in a family workshop during summer school recess
5   Laces on display in a shop window
6   A laces shop
7   A Brazilian client in conversation with Gurao agents and a representative from an underwear factory outside Vienna Hotel
8   Traditional courtyard houses in Gurao

6

7

8

Gurao, scale 1:10,000

Drift Trigger Two:

Figura-
tion

Figuration

Figuration, as the foundation of the Chinese "thought-language," is a force both deeply rooted and far-reaching; it is what orders things in Chinese cities, and grounds them in moral and aesthetic values. It is the Chinese culture's organizational principle in place of a "structure"—mathematical laws, religious orders, political systems, and knowledge disciplines—that shapes urban developments in the European and American contexts. This is not to say that intellectual reflections on numbers, spiritual life, governance, and knowledge do not exist in China; they are thought of differently.

The formative power and potential of figuration is perhaps best shown through the literati gardens in Suzhou. These gardens are nothing short of small versions of cosmological orders, and they are created by curating things such as land and water, rocks and vegetation, paths and architecture with great care. All things are placed in relation to one another and to the entirety but there are no explicit geometrical or structural schema in operation here. Instead, meticulous attention is brought to the shapes of things as figures (*xiang*) that stand for both a thing and a thought. The totality of effect takes place in the mind, in a way that is comparable to the Chinese language: its grammar is not in the language but in the mind, something that fascinated the thoughtful linguist Wilhelm von Humboldt as he wrote *On Language* (1836). Suzhou's literati gardens engage with moral and aesthetic values through what Humboldt described as a generality different from the specificity of the Greek mind. Figuration is the art of generality and structure is the art of specificity. Although the level of sophistication and beauty of figuration found in Suzhou gardens is rarely matched in popular and commercial developments in China today, it is important that we have this figurational aspiration in mind.

As figuration materializes in Chinese cities, two features emerge to contrast sharply with those in many Western cities: scale and authenticity. In the popular imagination, largeness of figures is often seen to be enormously empowering. Large size (*da*) is used frequently to mean greatness. The development of Chinese cities are critically shaped by this popular enthusiasm. In Shanghai's new urban areas of Lujiazui and Nanhui, human scale is clearly not the priority in urban design; instead, the heights of buildings and the largeness of the circle dictate relentlessly. Unlike cities such as Brasilia, this largeness of scale is hardly an aberration; from small cities such as Dongyang to major cities such as Hangzhou and Suzhou, their shiny new city centers are laid out as enormous and hastily curated things, spectacular from a distance but impossible for the pedestrian to walk in.

Authenticity is a much more complex and far-reaching conception. The main issue here is that authenticity is a highly cherished cultural construct of the Indo-European civilization, but its significance in China is limited. European philosophy's "metaphysics of presence" has meant the establishment of the condition of "being" in space and time. This, one may argue, is the intellectual grounding of the construct of the individual as the authentic being, one of the proudest achievements of the Indo-European civilization. In parallel, cities embody an authenticity of location, a sort of spirit of place (*genius loci*) paralleling the "spirit of person" (orality and being-in-the-world). This notion of the authentic location gave rise to the practice of pilgrimage—paying homage to the relic in its authentic location—that is rarely found in China. In the European and American urban context, inauthentic places can attain moral legitimacy as spaces of fantasy, permissible only in casinos and pleasure grounds. In China, recreating an exotic place in a different location has been a long-standing practice; in the seventeenth and eighteenth centuries, emperors in China recreated gardens they visited during their grand tours in their newly constructed pleasure grounds, and the Jesuits helped create European gardens as well. These were entirely untroubled by the moral discourse of authenticity and its moralizing language of fakery; the aesthetic delight is distinct from the connotation of deception. What is important here is to understand the relative role of the re-creation of exotic locations before quickly diving into the authenticity discourse. In the context of curating large urban areas in China, these recreated exotic places are very much part of a curatorial endeavor to effect some form of "completeness" or complementarity in a very large scheme. The fact that these were done with limited skills should not distract us from this understanding.

As shown in the examples of Thames Town, Minmetals Hallstatt, Hengdian, CIPEA (China International Practical Exhibition of Architecture), and Lujiazui, it is abundantly clear that this figurative curation of things has become an effective way to create real estate value. This accounts for the popularity of this approach, and it is grounded in the popular enthusiasm for figuration. These examples also demonstrate that the ways in which figuration works are complex and diverse. In Thames Town and Minmetals Hallstatt, the re-creation of attractive sites in distant locations is explicit. In Nanjing, in the development area known as CIPEA, figuration turns the avant-garde house from a symbol of criticality to a collected object, transforming, if not perverting, its cultural role. In Hengdian, the construction of famed sites in China provided value of place: storytelling, tourism, entertainment, commerce, and filmmaking all take place there as a site of multiple temporal frameworks. Shanghai's new central business district Lujiazui encapsulates the all-consuming desire to curate a list of modern and luxurious architectural items assembling an impressive skyline to be seen as a visual spectacle from across the Huangpu River; it has been a powerful driving force in Shanghai's urban planning and architecture.

As examples of figuration, the gulf between the literati gardens in Suzhou and the myriad of real estate development schemes illustrate a mental space in need of care. China's architectural education has neglected figuration; instead, for over a century and for good reason, it turns its attention to the understanding of the Western city. Chinese urbanization in the past four decades has highlighted the enduring resilience of China's "thought-language"; it is only with intellectual care that Chinese figuration can aspire to equal and surpass the enormous achievements of Suzhou gardens.

Shanghai   Songjiang   Thames Town

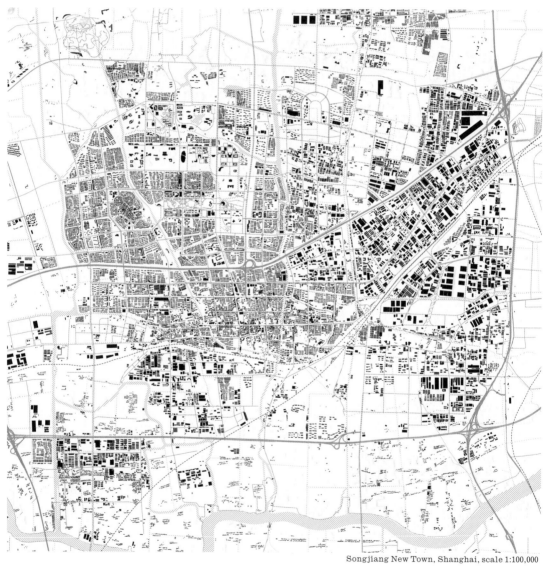

Songjiang New Town, Shanghai, scale 1:100,000

Thames Town:
The Lives of Others

Imagining and acting out the lives of others enriches cultural lives significantly; in eighteenth-century Europe, it seems that no palaces would be considered complete without at least a Chinese room. That eighteenth-century European fascination with the lives of others, before turning into Orientalism in the nineteenth century, gradually branched out into three separate directions: museums took up the curation of empirical facts of cultures, anthropology transformed the voyeuristic gaze into respectable scholarship, and amusement parks and casinos captured the fun factor. The complexity of experiencing the lives of others is perhaps best materialized through the folly in the garden—like William Chamber's pagoda at Kew Gardens (figure 1)—as a contrived otherness delightfully arranged in a distance.

Figure 1: A View of the Wilderness, with the Alhambra, the Pagoda, and the Mosque, drawing by W. Marlow, engraving by E. Rooker, 1763, The British Library

The folly as a way to imagine and act out the lives of others highlights an unspoken commitment to authenticity. Authenticity, as one of the most central moral values of the Indo-European civilization, is constructed in one important way as the authenticity of locations. *Genius loci*, the Roman framework of this connection between authenticity and location, has been an influential guiding principle for architectural and urban design. This is why ruins make sense as aesthetic objects in Europe;

they speak authenticity through their ruinous states.[1] When it comes to the moral values of authenticity, capitalism—and the industrial revolutions it demands—has been the single most profound source of anxiety in the twentieth century, as the division of labor seems to have undermined a presumed authentic experience of human lives. Karl Marx first raised the prospect of an alienation of human life, a critique that has remained a fixed feature in critical theory. Walter Benjamin reflected the disappearance of aura in art through mechanical reproduction, Hannah Arendt thought that repetitive and specialized labor reduces humans into a state of animal existence, and Adorno and Horkheimer cast doubt on the process of rationalization that led to consumerism as an inauthentic way of life. This deep concern for the evaporation of authenticity—all that is solid melts into air—frames a critical angle toward human lives constructed as simulacra, the most convincing example of which seems to be the symbolic and simulated lives in consumer society.[2] Imagining and acting out the lives of others is unmistakably framed in these terms in European and American cities.

It is one thing to have Paris or Venice fantastically recreated in Las Vegas, it is quite another to see an English town built in Shanghai as a real living community. Completed in 2006, Thames Town in Shanghai, in this critical frame of mind, seems to be the absurd culmination of the consumer society in its construction of simulacra. But Thames Town is situated in a culture that does not conceive the authenticity and folly dichotomy. To its residents, visitors, and the newlyweds having their photographs taken, Thames Town is a serious project and not a folly; it was designed by a British architectural firm Atkins, with its church modeled after Christ Church, Clifton Down in Bristol, and its pubs modeled after Lyme Regis, Dorset, and the Cross in Chester.

What does the Chinese culture conceive if not the authenticity and folly dichotomy? Fei Xiaotong, one of the most astute observers of the Chinese culture, tells us that it conceives a more distributed notion of the

It is one thing to have Paris or Venice fantastically recreated in Las Vegas, it is quite another to see an English town built in Shanghai as a real living community.

human through a framework that may be described as "other-encompassed self."[3] Authenticity is a consequence of a self sharply defined in opposition to others (other humans and nonhumans); this develops into a social, political, and economic framework of utilitarian individualism, one that now dominates most of the world, and that produces a normative critique of Thames Town as an inauthentic copy. Other-encompassed self is a cosmologi-

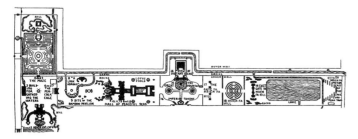

Figure 2: Sketch plan of the Western Mansions of Yuanmingyuan, from Carroll Brown Malone, *History of the Peking Summer Palaces under the Ch'ing Dynasty*, 1966

cal framework that conceives subjectivity and objectivity simultaneously, seeing the world as if from a third eye (neither subjective nor objective). This perhaps explains the surprise of Emperor Qianlong (1711–1799) when he first encountered European perspective paintings presented by the Jesuits: how strange, he reflected, that they choose to represent the flaw of the eye that makes parallel lines vanish into one point. Other-encompassed self, instead of fear and antagonism toward others, incorporates a reflexivity in general outlook to include "all beauties." The broad philosophical roots for this view can be found in founding theories of Chinese cosmology in the *Book of Changes*, Laozi, and Confucius; these contrast greatly with strategies of self-identification in Western cultures. The broad scheme of self-others distribution lies in the conception of ten thousand things (*wanwu*) that partake in the formation of any individual. In aesthetic practice, ten thousand things are presented as ten thousand figures (*wanxiang*), capturing the intertwining of self and others. As much as the Western city is an instrument of utilitarian individualism with its individualistic authenticity, protection of property rights, and socialization, the Chinese city assembles its ten thousand things aesthetically with much less distinct human-nature divide, investing its political and economic strategies in this scheme.

The Chinese experience of others is much more holistic than museum curation, the anthropological gaze, and amusement; it is made of all these and an inclination to create endless mutually complementary pairs as moral and aesthetic experience. In this sense, Thames Town is a popular attempt to capture the Chinese experience of others; we can perhaps understand the forces behind Thames Town through a better known example, Qianlong's expansion of the imperial pleasure garden in Beijing in 1760. Qianlong presided over one of the most prosperous periods in Chinese history, and he had been expanding the imperial pleasure garden Yuanmingyuan since his ascension to the throne in 1735. But the 1760 expansion is distinctive; he made use of a small strip of land at the northeast corner of this enormous garden (350 hectares) and named it Western Mansions (*xiyang lou*, figure 2). Western Mansions recreated European Baroque architecture and fountains with the help of Jesuits based in Beijing, Giuseppe Castiglione, Michel Benoist, and Jean Denis Attiret who reconstituted the design from different European architectural treatises they brought with them (figure 3). Qianlong's pleasure garden is an all-encompassing universe of ten thousand things: containing 123 groups of buildings (650 individually named structures) that created distinctive scenes and poetic writings; the six European "mansions," three fountains, a labyrinth, and a bridge were situated in Yuanmingyuan as components of a cosmological construction of mutually productive elements.[4]

Figure 3: Yuanmingyuan, engraving, 1783–1786. Commissioned by the Qianlong emperor and based on designs by Yi Lantai

The entire Yuanmingyuan, one may argue, is made of garden scenes that Qianlong, as well as emperors Kangxi and Yongzheng, collected over many decades from Southern China, where gardens were renowned. Qianlong

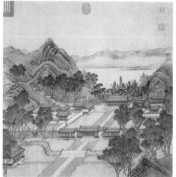

Figure 4: Shen Yuan, Tang Dai, one of 40 scenes and poems of Yuanmingyuan, 1744; poems were composed by Qianlong emperor.

made several tours of the South, admired deeply the southern gardens, and had them replicated for his imperial garden. In addition, he commissioned a collection of paintings and poems of 40 scenes of the Yuanmingyuan, with each scene painted on one side of a page and a poem on the other side (figure 4). Even this collection of 40 scenes is a re-creation of an iconic 31 scenes of Zhuozhengyuan in Suzhou painted and calligraphed by Wen Zhengming in 1533 (figure 5).

Figure 5: Wen Zhenming, one of 31 scenes and poems depicting Zhuozhengyuan, 1533

The Englishness of Thames Town, despite its hasty construction and anxious appeal to the popular taste, is much closer to the precedent of Qianlong's pleasure garden; Thames Town was part of a much larger scheme of one city, nine new cities, 60 small towns, and six hundred villages comprising Shanghai's overall strategy of urban expansion. The lives of others in Shanghai are not what they appear in the context of authenticity and folly; this understanding should not be distracted by circumstances of urgency, finance, and construction.

1
Li Shiqiao, "Memory without Location," *Understanding the Chinese City*, London: Sage Publications, 2014.
2
Jean Baudrillard, *The Consumer Society*, London: Sage Publications, 1970/1998.
3
Fei Xiaotong, "Reconsidering Human-Nature Relationships in Theories of Culture," *On Anthropology and Cultural Reflexivity*, Beijing: Huaxia Chubanshe, 2004.
4
Sun Dazhang, *Zhongguo gudai jianzhu shi*, volume 5, Beijing: Zhongguo Jianzhu Gongye Chubanshe, 2002, pp 89–98. Strassberg, Richard E., "War and Peace: Four Intercultural Landscapes," *China on Paper: European and Chinese Works from the Late Sixteenth to the Early Nineteenth Century*, edited by Marcia Reed and Paola Demattè, Los Angeles: Getty Publications, 2007, p.106.

William Chamber, pavilion and pagoda designs
Elevations, scale 1:350

China as Britain's other, Britain as China's figure

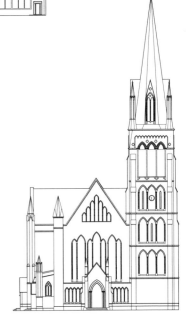

Selected buildings, Thames Town
Elevations, scale 1:700

Thames Town, scale 1:5,000

1   Thames Cathedral
2   Chinese hotpot restaurant
3   Townhouses in the town center

4

5

6

4   "Hotel de la Côte" carving out a French-inspired corner
in the English town on Holiday Square
5   A tailor shop offering British clothing
6   Victoria Street sign
7   Harry Potter statue at Municipal Pedestrian Street

7

1

2

3

4

5

1–2   Visitors taking photographs
3   Professional styled personal photography
4   Kayaking in the canal along Thames Town
5   Visitors on Holiday Square in front of the kayaking
ticket office
6   Professional styled personal photography

6

7

8

9

7   The founding date of Thames Town on a Kensington Gardens apartment building
8   Laundry outside the English townhouse
9   Apartment building overlooking the cathedral
10   Kensington Gardens residential area

10

1

1 Multiple wedding photography sessions on the lawn in front
of the Thames Cathedral
2 Wedding photography ateliers
3 Multiple wedding photography sessions on the street

2

3

4

5

6

7

4 Thinker Cafe and Bar and entrance to underground wedding photography studios
5 Photography set with romantic garden scenery in the underground wedding photography studios
6 Corridor with entrances to various self-service themed photography studios
7 Photography set with French-inspired night scene
8 Advertisement for the underground wedding photography studios promising British-styled settings without having to leave China

8

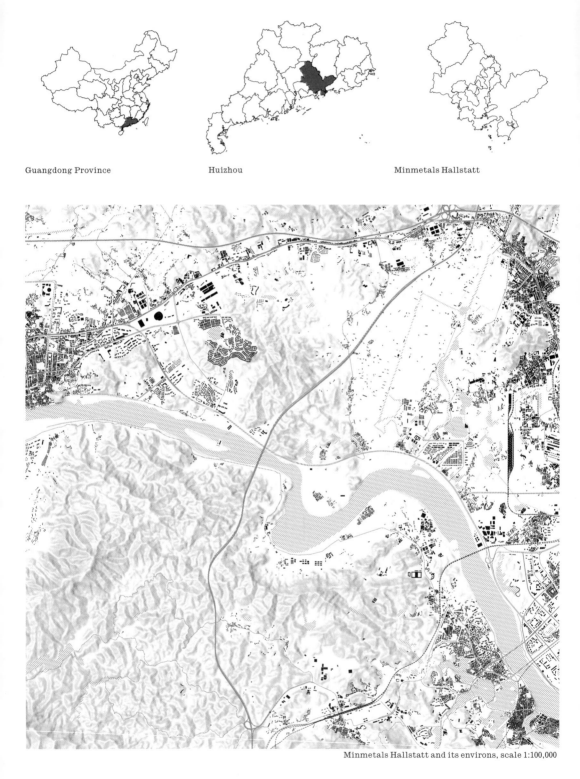

Guangdong Province

Huizhou

Minmetals Hallstatt

Minmetals Hallstatt and its environs, scale 1:100,000

Minmetals Hallstatt:
Gaming the Real Estate

Minmetals Hallstatt in Huizhou is more than copying a picturesque Austrian lakeside village, a UNESCO World Heritage Site (figure 1); it underscores the story of the high-pressure game of real estate in China as a foundational component in Chinese urbanization. Although Minmetals is a prestigious state-owned enterprise established in 1950 (one year after the founding of the People's Republic), its real estate subsidiary Minmetals Land was only established in 1993. From 1950s to today, Minmetals has grown to be a giant corporation, establishing a virtual monopoly in mining and minerals in China, and expanding to own a number of mines such as Las Bambas Copper Mine in Peru, Dugald River Zinc Mine in Australia, and Ramu Nickel and Colbalt Mine in Papua New Guinea. It is among the global top 10 mining companies in terms of output. In addition to mining and minerals, the corporation has

Figure 1: Hallstatt in Austria, photograph by Nick Csakany, wikimedia commons

expanded in areas such as trade and logistics, metallurgical engineering, finance, real estate, and construction. By 2018, the corporation managed a total asset of 1.85 trillion rmb, and had more than 200,000 employees. It is a Fortune 500 company (ranked 112 in 2019).[1]

The enormous strength of Minmetals Group does not readily translate into its real estate arm; Minmetals Land arrived at the scene with a relatively small portfolio. The Chinese real estate market is dominated by a long list of massive corporations both state-owned (such as China Poly

Group and Sunac China) and private (such as Evergrande Group and Vanke). Although lucrative, the Chinese real estate sector is fiercely competitive given the size and the number of players (China had approximately 95,000 real estate companies in 2016 according to the State Statistics Bureau). According to the real estate research firm CRIC, Minmetals Land ranked 105th in 2019 among China's real estate companies; it is one of the 16 state-owned real estate companies approved by the Chinese government to operate in the real estate market in China, although it is ranked relatively low among the 16.[2]

Minmetals Land faced additional challenges in 2010. In addition to the normative competition, China introduced tightening policies for the real estate market following a rapid rise of real estate prices resulting from stimulus brought in to offset the financial crisis in 2008.[3] One way to work around the state control was to develop in the area of tourist attractions (a sector that was still encouraged by the government around 2010); a flood of real estate projects were brought to realization by focusing on expanding the tourist capacity, be it

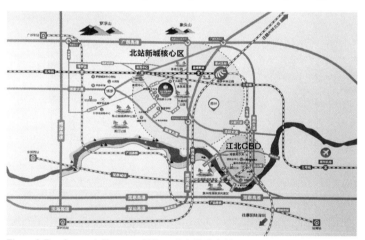

Figure 2: Development diagram of Minmetals Hallstatt area

eco-tourism or cultural tourism. As a real estate strategy, marketing an exotic architectural and life style has been a staple among Chinese real estate companies, following the precedent of Thames Town in Shanghai in 2004. In this context, Minmetals Land took two unusual decisions in 2010: to push for the "original taste" of an "exotic style" as the basic claim of tourist attraction, and to go for an Austrian style, which had not been used often by other Chinese developers. From the beginning,

Minmetals Hallstatt bet heavily on its tourist destination status.

Figure 3: Rendering of real estate development of Minmetals Hallstatt

To achieve the goal of a tourist destination, Minmetals Land invested 6 billion rmb at a location believed to have great potential: close to the city of Huizhou north of Guangdong Province with projected development of high-speed rails, highways, light-rails and underground trains (figure 2). Minmetals Land conducted extensive research on Hallstatt, in a way no other Chinese real estate developer had done with their stylistic claims. Alexander Scheutz, mayor of Hallstatt, told the *New York Times* that five Chinese architects arrived at Hallstatt in 2011 and recorded extensively.[4] Netease reported that Minmetals Land conducted infrared scans of the Hallstatt area onboard of an airplane to obtain precise topographical information in order to reproduce it faithfully in Huizhou.[5] Their efforts seem to have paid off; in 2015, Minmetals Hallstatt was granted a 4A (highest is 5A) tourist attraction status by the National Tourism Administration.

Figure 4: Model showing lightly Austrian-styled houses around Hallstatt Lake...

But the "Hallstatt" in Huizhou is made of only a fragment of Hallstatt in Austria, consisting of about 30 buildings forming a church square and a town square; its area of about 10,000 square meters is about 1 percent of the entire development area of 1 million square meters (figure 3). Although the "Hallstatt" in Huizhou aims at fidelity (minus the cultural dislocation that turns a *bäckerei* into a noodle shop), the rest of the development in the form of townhouses, villas, and residential highrises are only minimally styled with isolated signifiers of Alpine architecture (figures 4 and 5). Units are sold without

Figure 5: ...and in the podium levels of the residential towers

interior fitting out; the first added features of many of the residents are Chinese-style metal doors and prominent couplets surrounding the doors. Minmetals Hallstatt is one of a series of developments by Minmetals Land called "towns with characters," which include a Scottish Town in Changsha. This is in addition to a portfolio of other series of developments: the "golden city" series of inner city prestigious properties, "orchard pleasure" series of low-rise urban sites, "high-end" series of classic high-end real estate, and "ten thousand aspects" series of large-scale mid-range urban developments. Minmetals Land's portfolio, understandably, is diversified; it reflects a general trend in Chinese real estate design that appeals to nostalgia, ecology, exoticism, and hyper-modernity.[6]

It is worth stressing again that the moral discourse of authenticity—constructed implicitly in the language of real/fake, original/copied, and authentic/deceptive as judgmental categories—thwarts an understanding Minmetals Hallstatt deserves.

Like in the case of Thames Town in Shanghai, the occupation rate of Minmetals Hallstatt does not seem to be high and the town center certainly lacks the liveliness that is typically found in many cities in China. The units, however, appear to have been mostly sold as investments. Investors seem to be attracted by the prestige and strength of the parent company. Equally important, they are drawn toward the potential increase of real estate value; this is clearly presented by the real estate sales office at Minmetals Hallstatt: the completion of the high-speed rail stations, highways, light-rails, and underground trains, as well as its 4A tourist attraction status will in the near future drive the real estate value up. This is, it is stressed endlessly, what took place with Shenzhen's real estate market; those who bought early in Shenzhen are now enjoying an enormous return on investment.

Minmetals Land and its Hallstatt project may be a catchy headline in popular media, the contexts of its development tell a familiar tale of China's urbanization: the psychology of investors, the pecking order of developers, the ruthless competition in a lucrative market, and the strategic use of exotic cultures to game the real estate regulations. It is worth stressing again that the

moral discourse of authenticity—constructed implic-
itly in the language of real/fake, original/copied, and
authentic/deceptive as judgmental categories—thwarts
an understanding Minmetals Hallstatt deserves; a concept
of simulacrum is part of the concept of authenticity. In
Minmetals Hallstatt, this "authenticity anxiety" never
emerged to guide its production; instead, it was the
pleasure of figuration—for both the developer and the
buyer—that led them to the unprecedented pursuit of
accuracy. Neither an empirical documentation, nor an
anthropological gaze, nor a pleasure ground, Minmetals
Hallstatt is a figurated object curated in a high stakes
game of real estate speculation.

1
http://www.minmetals.com/english/
about_666/AboutMinmetals/
2
https://finance.sina.com.cn/
chanjing/cyxw/2019-03-20/
doc-ihsxncvh4069529.shtml
3
https://m.21jingji.com/article/20170308/
herald/de05b5a62fa388f7d4dbaaf53418a36c.
html
4
https://www.nytimes.com/2012/07/26/
world/europe/26iht-letter26.html
5
Reported by Netease reporters
Ou Jiayan and Li Xu, July 2,
2012, at http://sz.house.163.
com/12/0702/18/85E9051R00074KD1.
html#p=85E89PS12AJR0007
6
Daniel Sui, Bo Zhao, Hui Kong,
"The Development of Copycat Towns
in China," Working Paper, Lincoln
Institute of Land Policy, 2017.

Three place-making strategies: linguistic signs at Aspern
Seestadt, simulacrum at Celebration, figuration at
Minmetals Hallstatt
Scale 1:10,0000

Celebration
Florida, USA

Aspern Seestadt
Vienna, Austria

Minmetals Hallstatt
Guangdong Province, China

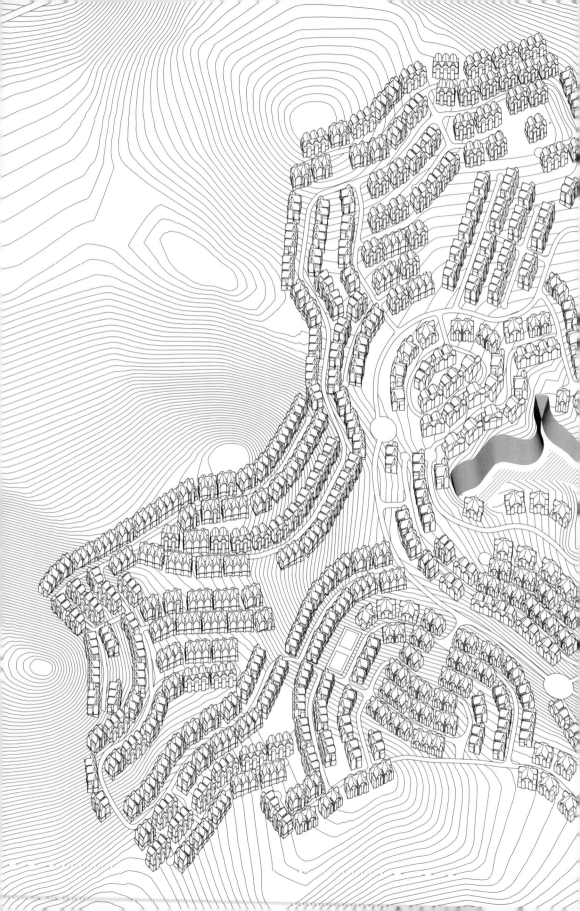

Minmetals Hallstatt, scale 1:5,000

1 Bridge leading to the part of Minmetals Hallstatt, which is a
replica of the Austrian town of Hallstatt
2 Visitor center employees wearing traditional Austrian *dirndl*
3 Street with cafes in the replicated center
4 Visitors taking photographs in front of the Austria Center

5

5   Real estate showroom
6   View onto the lake
7   View toward completed phase two of houses, and phase two
of highrises under construction
8   Interior of the church, which is used for real estate sales events

6

7

8

1 Phase one houses on the cliff overlooking the "Austrian Town"
2 Lightly Austrian-styled residences lined with palm trees
3 Re-creation of the timber roof construction of Austrian houses through in-situ concrete
4 Chinese couplets framing entrances to the houses
5 View across phase two of houses toward the lake and the "Austrian Town" from a highrise apartment building of phase two under construction
6 View down onto the entrance and parking lot of a semi-detached house
7 Residential street with view toward phase two of highrises under construction
8 Austrian-styled facade treatment of the podium of phase two residential highrise buildings

1

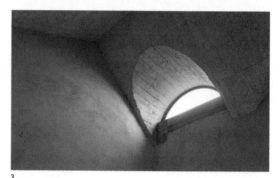

2

3

4

5

6

7

8

Zhejiang Province   Dongyang   Hengdianzhen

Hengdian, scale 1:100,000

Hengdian:
The Production of Time

Seeing from our habitual singular, homogenous framework of space and time, Hengdian seems surreal. Yet, it
is far from a Borgesian construct; it is an urban reality
that needs to be understood outside the peculiarity of a
singular space-time mental construct. Hengdian is a 5A
tourist attraction certified by China's National Tourism
Administration, equal in status to the world-renowned
historical-tourist sites such as the Great Wall and Suzhou
gardens. Hengdian's 5A status was obtained without a
single site of historical origin; it was based on near full
scale reproductions of a range of historical sites elsewhere, many—like the Des Voeux Road in Hong Kong and
the palace of the first emperor of China in Xi'an —are no
longer recognizable or exist today. Hengdian is part of the
city of Dongyang, Zhejiang Province, and has a population of about 180,000. In 2018, Hengdian received 329 film
crews and 14.3 million tourists, resulting in an income of
23.5 billion rmb. In total, Hengdian hosted more than 2,100
film crews making 54,000 films/episodes; costume dramas
made in Hengdian make up two-thirds of all production
in China.[1] Filming on site for production teams is free of
charge; Hengdian profits from the provision of hospitality,
services, extras (known as the Hengdian Drifters, or *hengpiao*), and rental of equipment, costumes, and horses.

Figure 1: *The Opium War*, directed by Xie Jin, Emei Film Studio / Golden Harvest
Mandarin Films, 1997

Hengdian's economic rise is not too different from
many other small towns in rural China. In the 1970s,
Hengdian was known as a place to "endure hunger with
thin congee"; lacking in fertile agricultural land and

surrounded by hills, Hengdian struggled to find a viable economic life. Xu Wenrong (1935-) led Hengdian to seek employment in establishing a silk factory in the 1980s, beginning a series of experiments in production types that ranged from magnets, to drugs, to animal feed.[2] His big break came in 1996, six years after he established Hengdian Group, a rather paternalistic all-encompassing umbrella organization made of 60 companies that provided not only employment but also social welfare such as schools and

While the past is ever-present in Hengdian, it is nevertheless not a place for history.

hospitals. In 1996, to celebrate the historic event of the handover of Hong Kong to China, the renowned Chinese film director Xie Jin looked for a location to make an epic film, *The Opium War* (figure 1). Frustrated with the difficulties of constructing a film set in bigger cities such as Shanghai and Hangzhou, Xie Jin came across Xu Wenrong who built the film set, the now popular Guangzhou Street, in record time. This fortuitous encounter with Xie Jin and the making of *The Opium War* set Hengdian in a direction no one anticipated: tourism. With nothing distinctive in its natural terrain, Xu was convinced that he could build "sceneries." He achieved far more than just tourism.

Hengdian constructed 28 projects and film sets since the completion of Guangzhou Street, creating a network of diverse sites that now define the city of Hengdian more than anything from its own history. Following the construction of Guangzhou Street, the Qin Palace became the next successful project; here the epic *The Emperor and The Assassin* by Chen Kaige in 1997 (figure 2), and *Hero* by Zhang Yimou in 2001 (figure 3) are two of the blockbuster movies that helped propel Chen and Zhang to international stardom. Encouraged by these initial successes, Hengdian went on to build Hong Kong Street (a reconstruction of the nineteenth-century Des Voeux Road), Along the River During the Qingming Festival (a creation of a Song-dynasty city inspired by the eleventh-century scroll by Zhang Zeduan), and the Forbidden City in Beijing (with the original no longer being accessible to film crews since Bernardo Bertolucci's 1987 film *The Last Emperor*). Less well-known to tourists but important to Hengdian's sense of place-making is the Residential Houses of Ming and Qing Dynasties Museum, a reconstituted theme park

Figure 2: *The Emperor and the Assassin*, directed by Chen Kaige, Shin Corporation, Le Studio Canal+ / Sony Pictures Classics, 1997

Figure 3: *Hero*, directed by Zhang Yimou, Sil-Metropole Organisation / Beijing New Picture Film, Miramax Films, ETCO Film, 2001

made of largely original vernacular residential buildings from other parts of China, dismantled and reassembled in Hengdian.

Hengdian's transformation is accidentally and inextricably intertwined with the construction of these full-scale sites. European and American cities tend to stretch their production of time through a spectrum of ruins (Acropolis in Athens) to simulations (Universal Studios in Los Angeles). While ancient thoughts of time are multi-dimensional (Greek time was cyclical, Greek and Christian gods were "omnipresent"), the invention of history since the sixteenth century imposed a singular and homogenous time that renders the past "historical." Any form of reappearance of the past—like a reconstructed historical site—will have to take place in special places such as amusement parks and casinos; its cultural status is rather dubious, as attested by the concepts of Foucault's *heterotopia* and Baudrillard's *simulacra*. The normative building of cities in Europe and America are concerned with the building of the present, made possible by the simultaneous practice of "historic preservation."

Hengdian combines "authenticity" (reassembled and relocated original residences), filmmaking, entertainment, and knowledge of the past into one operation, resetting the foundation of the city away from its agricultural life in an average and unremarkable location to a place best known for its tourist sites. While the past is ever-present in Hengdian, it is nevertheless not a place for history. There are three kinds of past that confront visitors. First is the past architectural forms that are dislocated, as in the Residential Houses of Ming and Qing Dynasties Museum. Second is the reconstructed and reconstituted architectural past no longer extant, as in the Qin Palace. Third is the past filmic narratives that have since become iconic cultural experiences, with their key scenes filmed in specific locations in Hengdian. All these layers seem to merge into each other as visitors move through the reconstructed and reconstituted spaces, drifting from lessons in history to adoration of film stars. Tourist guides seem to have no difficulty in conveying these layers of past blended together in continuous narratives. This is not an alternative to a real Hendian; this is Hengdian in all its capacities.

Figure 4: *I Am Somebody*, directed by Derek Yee, Zhejiang Bona Film and Television Production, Huaxia Film Distribution, Distribution Workshop, 2015

One of the most interesting aspects of urban life in Hengdian concerns its extras, the *hengpiao*. Nearly 48,200 of them are registered with the Hengdian World Studios Actors Union. Migrating from other parts of China to Hengdian in search of a career and stardom, *hengpiaos* typically live in cheap accommodations and use social media to seek appearances in films. They are compensated by the number and type of appearances; finding opportunities to be cast as an extra is crucial. There are two main gathering places for *hengpiaos*: the Service Center of the Hengdian World Studios Actors Union and Hengpiao Square, a small urban park at the center of the city. The Hengdian extra's claim to fame is the 2015 film *I Am Somebody* (figure 4) directed by the Hong Kong director Derek Yee, who used primarily real *hengpiaos* to tell a love story set in the context of the lives and struggles of migrant extras in Hengdian.

Hengdian is indicative of a production of time in multiple dimensions: in storytelling, amusement, cultural identity formation, nationalism, and locating authenticity. Instead of pursuing an ideal construct of singular and homogenous time, Hengdian's production of time reflects the various temporal constructs in daily lives, un-policed by the disciplines of history and historiography.

In this sense, Hengdian's production of time parallels
the thing-based intellectual framework, as we formulate
through the notion of figuration, that grants legitimacy to
multiple temporal frameworks. What we have in Hengdian
is similar to what we experience in Suzhou gardens, only
that the multiple temporal frameworks in Suzhou gardens
were brought to materiality with great care and cultivation of the *literati*. Hengdian's unmitigated enthusiasm
for the most accessible forms of pleasure does not have to
limit the potential of this approach to city making; there
are resources for intellectual insights and aesthetic richness in the simultaneous existence of multiple temporal
frameworks. Having never been modern, Hengdian seems
to never have conceived a notion of homogenous time.

1
Report by Wu Shuaishuai for
Xinhuanet, http://www.xinhuanet.com/
politics/2018-12/04/c_1123807211.htm.
2
Xu Wenrong, *Solving the Difficult
Problems of the Century* (pojie shiji
nanti), private printing, 2003.

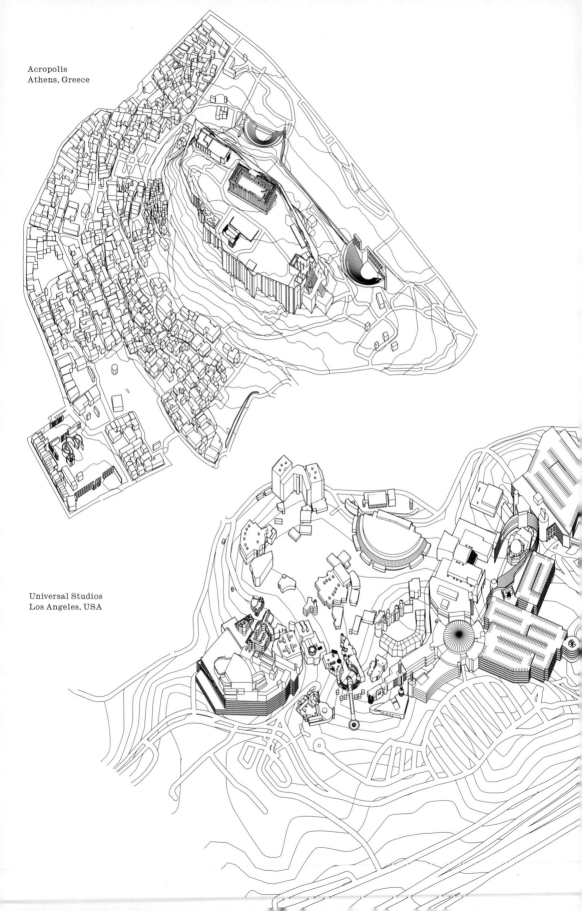

Acropolis
Athens, Greece

Universal Studios
Los Angeles, USA

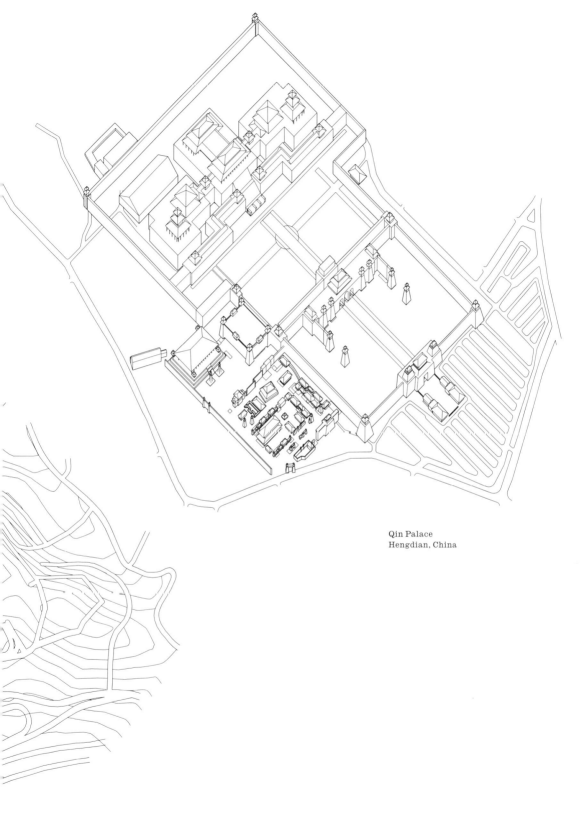

Qin Palace
Hengdian, China

Historical time at Athens, fantastical time at Universal Studios,
timeless time at Hengdian's Qin Palace, scale 1:60,000

Hengdian, scale 1:7,500

Guangzhou Street and Hong Kong Street Scenic Area

The first filming location built in Hengdian comprises a reconstruction of nineteenth-century Guangzhou (built in 1996) including Sanyuanli Street, Thirteen Factories, and Shamian. In 1998, a reconstruction of early twentieth-century Hong Kong was added, including Victoria Harbour, Connaught Road, Queens Road, Statue Square, HSBC Bank, and St. John's Cathedral.

1

2

3

1 Guangzhou Street
2 Tianlan Tea Pavilion
3 Children extras in action

4

5

6

7

4   Show "Master and Commander," staged for visitors
5   Replica of St. John's Cathedral in Hong Kong Central
6   Workers preparing a new film set
7   Tourist group led by an official guide from Hengdian
World Studios
8   Looking across Statue Square and the stairs of HSBC Bank in
Hong Kong Street scenic area. The set is prepared for filming with
costumes for extras.

8

Qin Dynasty Palace

This impressive film set is a re-creation of a palace complex from the second century BCE, with two large courtyards formed by a range of buildings and walls. The buildings are constructed from a mix of materials ranging from real stone and bricks to plastic and fiber glass imitations of these materials. The set has acted as a backdrop for countless films, including *The Emperor and the Assassin* and *Hero*.

1

1   Approaching the gate of the Qin Dynasty Palace
2   A camouflage wall is being erected as a service space for film crews.
3   The Hall of the Union of Four Seas where the emperor presides; one of the most popular filming locations for historical dramas
4   A horse waits for its appearance in filming. Hengdian has a large horse rental operation supporting the needs of historical battles in films.
5   A photo corner with green screen for visitors to take photographs in costumes and with a historical background of their choice
6   A girl posing for photo taking in a historical dress
7   View across the Double Channel between the two courtyards

2

3

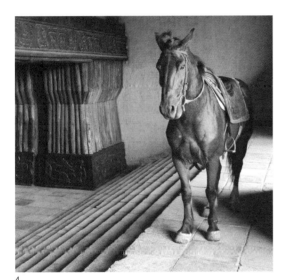

4

5

6

7

Residential Houses of Ming and Qing Dynasties

The main attraction of this theme-park-like area is its collection of residential houses of Ming and Qing dynasties that
have been dismantled and reassembled from various parts of
China. They are supplemented by replicas of historic residential houses to make this area complete, serving the functions
of both tourist attraction and film set. Unlike the Guangzhou
Street and Hong Kong Street Scenic Area and the Qin Dynasty
Palace, this location does not replicate a specific place, but
offers a generic traditional backdrop.

View from the Bridge of Literature and Virtue

1   Historic residences from Fang Village in Anhui Province,
dating back to the Qing dynasty, migrated to Hengdian in 2003.
2   Interior view of one of the courtyard buildings
3   Filming in progress
4   View toward Cheng De Hall, which was built in Anhui
Province during the Qing dynasty in 1882, and relocated to
Hengdian in 2004.
5   Wu Yi Street, originally located in Lu Tan Village in Zhejiang
Province, dating back to the Qing dynasty. In 2004 it was moved
to Hengdian.

Hengdian City Center

The city center of Hengdian is dominated by two buildings, the headquarter of Hengdian Group, and the headquarter of its main subsidiary, Hengdian World Studios. Hengdian Group has a wide ranging business operation, from electronics to pharmaceutical and chemical industries, to film and entertainment. Hengdian World Studios manages its most successful operation. The success of the film and entertainment industry is reflected in the conversion of Wang Sheng South Street, the address of Hengdian World Studios, into a pedestrian zone that is themed as a film set of an early twentieth-century Shanghai urban scene.

The pedestrian zone in Wang Sheng South Street with the clock tower of Hengdian World Studios Headquarters (left), and Hengdian Group Headquarters in Baixan Street (right)

Right
Hengdian City Center, scale 1:1,000

1

2

3

1   A gate leading to the pedestrian zone in Wang Sheng South
Street marked as "Wang Sheng Films"
2   A layer of early twentieth-century Shanghai shop signage
over the current actual shop names
3   A live social media broadcast using the pedestrian zone as a
"film set"
4   Just around the corner from Wang Sheng Street is Yuyang
Street, where daily commercial life takes place.
5   Film support businesses are concentrated in Qinming Riverside
Road and Denglong Road; here a post production studio, a
painting studio for film sets, and a casting company in Qinming
Riverside Road.
6   Looking into Qinming Riverside Road from Extras Square
7   Hengpiao Hotel (Hengdian Extras Hotel) renamed from
Wanhao Hotel, acknowledging the presence of the well-known
film extras in Hengdian
8   The nightmarket on Denglong Street frequented by
Hengdian extras
9   An extra posing in the Hengpiao Hotel lobby for a visitor

4

5

6

8

7

9

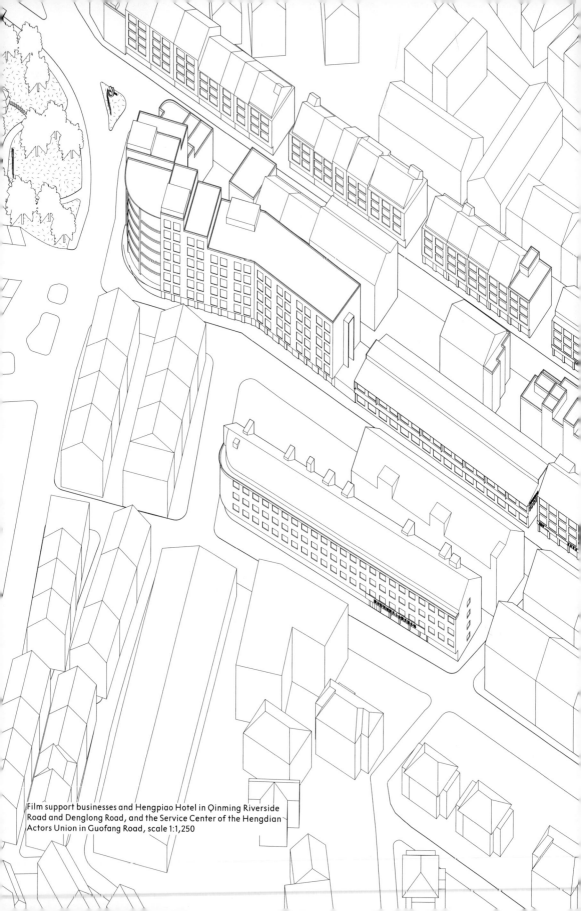

Film support businesses and Hengpiao Hotel in Qinming Riverside Road and Denglong Road, and the Service Center of the Hengdian Actors Union in Guofang Road, scale 1:1,250

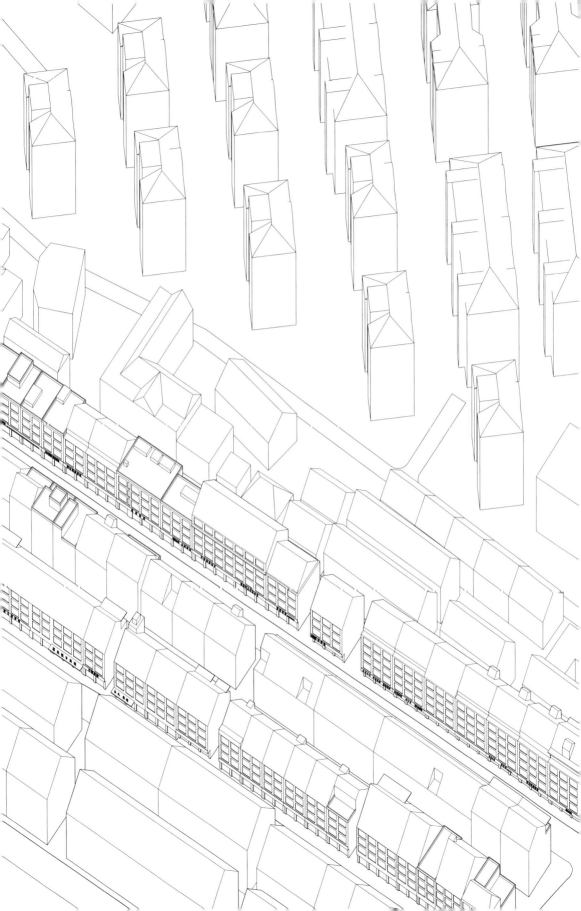

Hengdian World Studios Actors Union Service Center

The service center in Guofang Road is the first place to go for
aspiring actors who come to Hengdian from all over China.
Established in 2003, it centrally manages the welfare of
Hengdian extras through issuing of actors' identity cards.
These provide personal information to film crews and are
used to log appearances for which the extras are paid twice
a month. As of March 2016, 48,200 extras have been registered with the union. In 2016 alone, extras have accounted for
570,000 appearances in films produced in Hengdian.

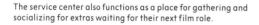

The service center also functions as a place for gathering and
socializing for extras waiting for their next film role.

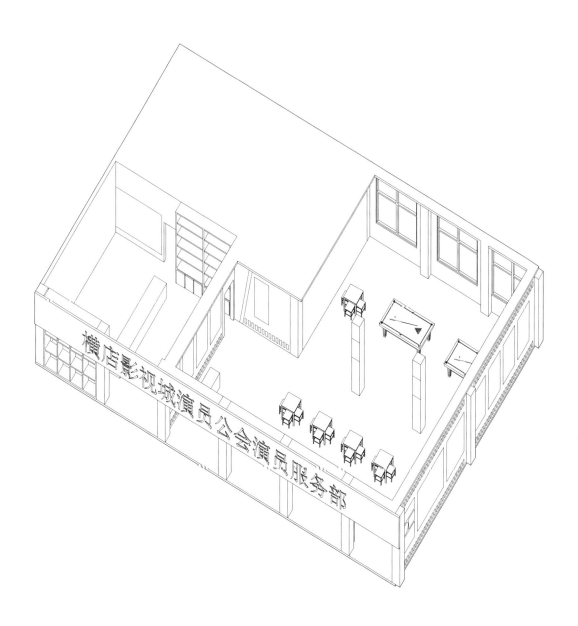

Hengdian World Studios Actors Union Service Center
Scale 1:200

Hengpiao Square

Hengpiao Square (Hengdian Extras Square) is another place
for extras to gather and socialize. It is located in proximity to
the Actors Union Service Center, providing a small range of
leisure and educational facilities. Information boards show-
case famous *hengpiaos* and announce training opportunites.
While currently extras are informed of their film roles through
social media platforms, the square was originally used for
film crews to recruit in person thus giving it an enduring reputation. Hengpiao Square featured prominently in the movie
I Am Somebody.

Four extras socializing while waiting for their next film roles

Right
Hengdian Extras Square, scale 1:750

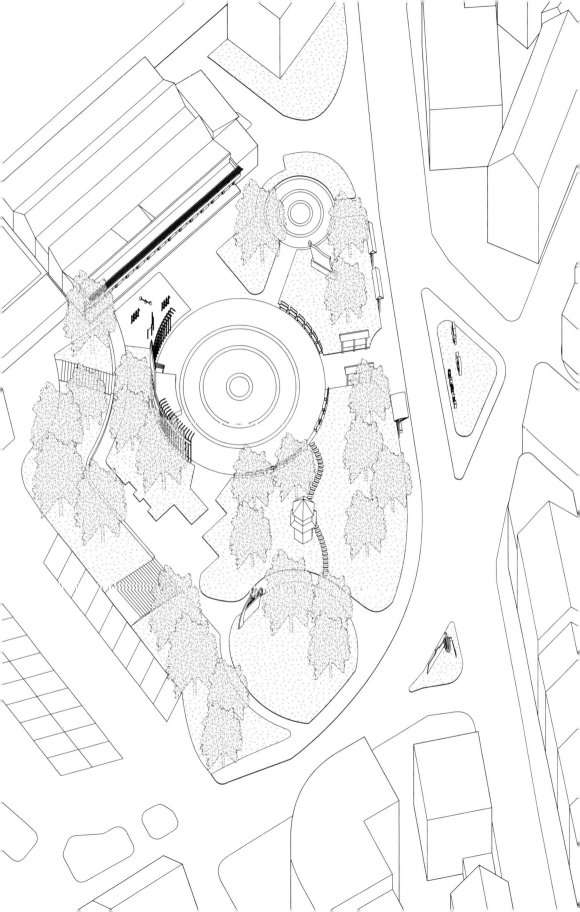

Jiangsu Province   Nanjing   CIPEA Foshouhu

Foshouhu and Nanjing, scale 1:100,000

CIPEA:
Avant-garde as Superfluous Things

There is a unique function for the avant-garde; it embodies what Bertrand Russell described as an enthusiasm that defies prudence, a Dionysian intoxication that disrupts an Apollonian educated caution. Russell argued that it is this Dionysian spirit that set the Western civilization apart and advanced its course. In architecture, this translates into a list of extraordinarily innovative buildings: Bramante's Tempietto, Palladio's Villa Rotunda, Burlington's Chiswick Villa, Mies van der Rohe's Barcelona Pavilion, Le Corbusier's Villa Savoye, Johnson's Glass House, Neutra's Kaufmann House, Venturi's Vanna Venturi House. These are part of a very long list but the narrative is relatively simple; for this reason, historians of architectural ideas labor on their cultural significance. Architectural history and theory, it seems, has built a symbiotic relationship with these projects, which sustain the architectural profession intellectually.

Figure 1: Commune by the Great Wall, built in 2000

The high cultural cachet of an extraordinary house design has not gone unnoticed in China, even though the centerpiece of a traditional Chinese house is a courtyard, not a villa. In 1995, a young economics graduate from Sussex University, Zhang Xin, established Soho China with her husband Pan Shiyi, and led a project in 2000 called Commune by the Great Wall (figure 1) on a piece of land of 8 square kilometers at the bottom of the Great Wall in

Beijing originally purchased to build a golf course. Zhang Xin persuaded her husband to create 100 "mountain whisper houses" following the European villa type.[1] She ended up inviting 12 prominent Asian architects to design 12 houses: Airport House by Chien Hsueh-Yi, Bamboo Wall by Kengo Kuma, Cantilever House by Antonio Ochoa, Clubhouse by Seung H-Sang, Distorted Courtyard House by Rocco Yim, Forest House by Nobuaki Furuya, Furniture House by Shigeru Ban, See and Seen House by Cui Kai, Shared House by Kanika R'kul, Split House by Yung Ho Chang, Suitcase House by Gary Chang, and the Twin House by Kay Ngee Tan. Shown at the Venice Biennale in 2002, it

They seem to be figures of avant-garde design rather than fulfillment of their cultural function as rebellious challenges to house norms.

stirred up a sensation in Chinese contemporary architecture due to the extraordinary combination of the Great Wall and the format of a cluster of house designs in Asia. It also gave rise to puzzlement: these "houses" have no clients, no briefs, and no cultural contexts; they seem to operate in a self-referential avant-garde houseness. They seem to be figures of avant-garde design rather than fulfillment of their cultural function as rebellious challenges to house norms.

In 2003, a father and son team, Lu Jun and Lu Xun of 4 Cube Cultural Industry Group (Sifang) in Nanjing, invited 12 Chinese architects and 12 international architects to begin developing a 0.4 square kilometer piece of land at the scenic Laoshan area in Nanjing, costing 660 million rmb. It is now known as CIPEA (China International Practical Exhibition of Architecture). In addition to doubling the number of architects compared with the Commune by the Great Wall, they have also expanded on building types: including an art gallery by Steven Holl, a hotel by Liu Jiakun, a conference center by Arata Isozaki, and a spa and recreation center by Ettore Sottsass. Wang Shu, Kazuyo Sejima, David Adjaye, Ai Weiwei, among others, contributed house designs. The development was planned to have two phases: first the 24 projects by invited architects, second a real estate scheme consisting of nine low-rise blocks of luxurious apartments called 24 Cubes (figure 2). CIPEA has quickly established a solid reputation as a development designed by "24 famous architects,"

Figure 2: The real estate brochure by Sunac advertising the 24 Cubes development within the context of the China International Exhibition of Architecture (CIPEA)

driving up the value of 24 Cubes significantly. It was purchased by the Chinese real estate behemoth Sunac in May 2015 as Sunac's foray into the real estate market in Nanjing; however, their larger goal to develop land parcels around CIPEA has been undermined by Nanjing's attempt to reign in construction in its valuable scenic areas such as Laoshan.

Numbers do not stop at 24. Among many attempts to reach the figurative number 100 in cultural productions, the most fascinating is the Museum Cluster Jianchuan (figure 3), a private enterprise established in 2003 by the self-styled "museum slave" Fan Jianchuan, who made his fortune in real estate. Passionate about collecting artifacts of the wars and revolutions in China, Fan resolved to build 100 museums in his lifetime; he purchased a piece of land of about one third of a square kilometer in the town of Anren in Sichuan Province to begin with 15 museums. This turned Anren into a "museum town." He built 40 museums by 2018 with a collection of over a billion artifacts costing 2 billion rmb.[2] Like the avant-garde house, the museum and its function to enable histories of cultural innovations have gone through deep re-contextualization: Fan Jianchuan describes his creation as a "supermarket of museums."[3]

Figure 3: Museum Cluster Jianchuan, tourist map

The endlessly irresistible attraction of the figurative number of 100 may seem excessive, but it has a deep cultural grounding; it manifests itself in bewildering varieties, such as 100 flowers, 100 sons, 100 horses, 100 chicken feast, etc. Shiqiao Li described this enduring feature in the Chinese culture as an imperative to abundance: a notion of the flourishing of life through specific numbers:[4] 10, 100, 1,000 are used to mark the flourishing of life, although 12 and 24 (numbers of months and solar terms) are also popular; 100 is pursued in great vigor since it is much more accomplished than 10 but much more realistic than 1,000. Each number, as the renowned eleventh-century thinker Shao Yong remarked, has its own "thingness," a magnitude that cannot be reduced by mathematical abstraction. This deep intellectual tradition grounds the nature of collections of precious objects—"superfluous things" as

Figure 4: 100 architects on their site visit in the desert of Ordos, courtesy of LTL Architects

Wen Zhenheng's iconic essay *Zhangwu Zhi* (*Treatise on Superfluous Things*, 1620–1627) frames them—that are so divergent from the conception of "cabinets of curiosities" in Europe.

In an extraordinary twist, the critical efficacy of 100 was brought out vividly in a performance piece—avant-garde turned into rear guard turned into avant-garde again—by Ai Weiwei in 2008. Ai Weiwei, in collaboration with Herzog de Meuron (they collaborated on the Beijing Olympic Stadium earlier), invited 100 young architects from around the world to design 100 villas in Ordos, Inner Mongolia, China. The irony of the avant-garde would hardly have escaped the keen critical eye of Ai Weiwei when he took part in CIPEA, contributing a house called Six Rooms. Ordos has one-sixth of China's coal reserves and the wealth from the coal mines was invested in a massive real estate scheme in an area called Kangbashi, with a capacity of one million inhabitants, built between 2005 and 2010. In 2017, it managed to attract about 100,000 inhabitants, perhaps not quite sufficient to exorcise its reputation as China's most dramatic "ghost city."[5] In 2008, Ordos was at the peak of its confidence to pull this development off; a private enterprise, Jiangyuan Water Engineering Ltd, sponsored the event and the mayor of Ordos was eager to support Ai Weiwei's proposal. Attracted by the prospect to build a house in China, the invited international architects were highly motivated. Enthusiasm soon turned into puzzlement: unlike CIPEA, Ordos has a distinctly surreal quality. Designing 100 enormous villas (1,000 square meters each) in the middle of a desert (figure 4) with no client and no context (all 100 architects drew a lottery that determined which site they were designing for), like in a game of *cadavre exquis*, triggered both excitement and panic. Ai Weiwei made a film, *Ordos 100* (2012), to document the entire process of dramatic emotional swings of architects outside their comfort zones. With Ai Weiwei, the power of 100 is turned from deep convention into radical provocation even though Ordos 100 remains unfinished today; Ai Weiwei, like Xu Bing and Zhan Wang, invented a Chinese criticality and a Chinese modernity that would no doubt lead to an important cultural development in the twenty-first century. For this development of criticality in Chinese architecture, the Commune by the Great Wall and CIPEA have laid down important foundations.

1
https://news.newseed.cn/p/1342024;
Zou Tongxian and Cui Hallei,
Classic Examples of Development and Management of Tourist Real Estate (lvyou dichan kaifa yu jingying jingdian anli)
Beijing: Beijing shefan daxue chubanshe, 2010.
2
http://www.jc-museum.cn/news/560.html
3
New York Times interview, https://cn.nytimes.com/culture/20130806/cc06fanjianchuan/
4
Li Shiqiao, *Understanding the Chinese City*, London: Sage Publications, 2014.
5
Matt Sheehan, *Huffington Post*, December 6, 2017.

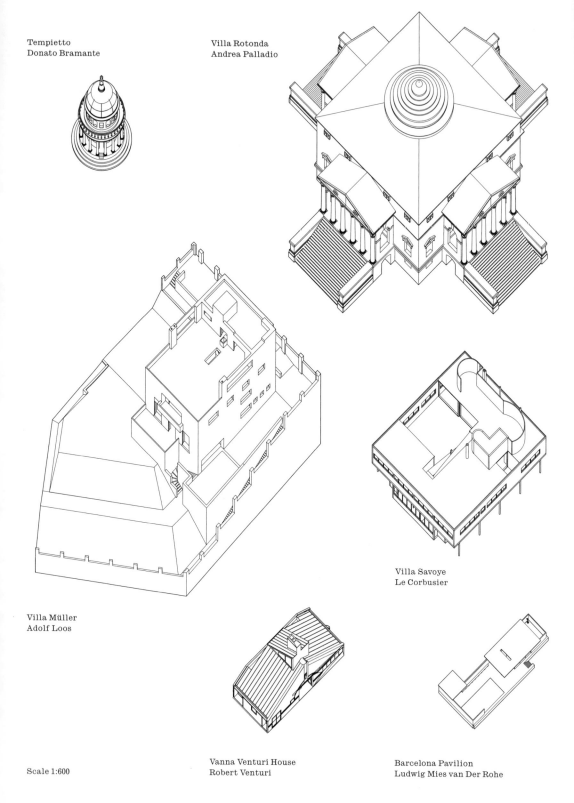

Tempietto
Donato Bramante

Villa Rotonda
Andrea Palladio

Villa Müller
Adolf Loos

Villa Savoye
Le Corbusier

Scale 1:600

Vanna Venturi House
Robert Venturi

Barcelona Pavilion
Ludwig Mies van Der Rohe

The house as the avant-garde: singular break-through cultural
events versus collections of exceptional aesthetic value

Commune by the Great Wall

Chien Hsueh-Yi, Kengo Kuma, Antonio Ochoa, Seung H-Sang, Rocco Yim, Nobuaki Furuya, Shigeru Ban, Cui Kai, Kanika R'kul, Yung Ho Chang, Gary Chang, Kay Ngee Tan

Ordos 100

Andreas Thiele Architekten / Ines Geisler Weizman Architecture; Territorial Agency; Alejandro Aravena; at103; Atelier Bow Wow; Babel Architects; Bachelard Wagner Architekten; Alexandra Barker; Tatiana Bilbao; Bill Price Inc.; Blacklinesonewhitepaper; Bottega + Ehrhardt Architekten; Buchner Bründler AG; Christ + Gantenbein; Christophe Hutin Architecture; Colboc & Franzen; Dieguez Fridman; Coll-Leclerc Arquitectos; constructconcept; Dellekamp Arquitectura; DRDH Architects; Efrat-Kowalsky Architects; Encore Heureux + G Studio; Estudio Barozzi Veiga; Frida Escobedo; F451arquitectura; FRENTEarquitectura; Sou Fujimoto; HA: SKA; Heiermann Architekten; HHF; IKstudio; Ines Huber; iwamotoscott; Jan De Vylder Architecten; JDS architects; Jean-Fréderic Luscher; Johnston Mark Lee Architects; JSa; JSA@Norway; Jun Igarashi Architects; Keller Easterling; Könz Molo Architects; L'Atelier Provisoire; Larnaudie Jean & Luc; Leon de Lima; Lekker Design; Ligia Nobre + Eduardo de Oliveira Rosa; Lost Architekten; LTL Architects; Luca Selva Architekten; Lyn Rice Architects; Makeka Designs; Manuel Herz Architecture; Mass Studies; Matharoo Associates; Mazzapokora; Mierta & Kurt Lazzarini Architects; Milica Topalovic—Bas Princen—Paul Gerretsen; Miller Maranta Architekten; Mimarlar Yapi Tasarim; MOS; Mühendislik ve Danismanlik Hizmetleri; Multiplicities; Toshiko Mori; NAO; n Architects; Nile Street Studios; NL Architects; NU architectuuratelier; OBRA Architects; Office Kersten Geers David Van Severen; Oyler Wu Collaborative; PAD; Pedrocchi Meier Architects; Polaris Architects; Preston Scott Cohen; Productora; Cecilia Puga; Adi Purnomo; R&Sie(n); Smiljan Radic; Rintala Eggertsson Architects; Pako Rodriguez; Rocker-Lange Architects; Rojkind Arquitectos; Sami Arquitectos; Matti Sanaksenaho; Rafi Segal; Senan Architects, Slade Architecture; Studio-sr; SSD; Taller Territorial de Mexico; Territorial Agency; Testbedstudio Architects; Tham & Videgård Hansson Arkitekter; UNI; weberbuess Architekten; WORKac; Adrian Zenin

CiPEA Foshou Lake

Steven Holl, Liu Jiakun, Arata Isozaki, Ettore Sottsass, Zhou Kai, Kazuyo Sejima and Ryue Nishizawa, Zhang Lei, Mathias Klotz, David Adjaye, Luis M. Mansilla and Emilio Tuñón, Sean Godsell, Odile Decq, Liu Heng, Philip F. Yuan, Wang Shu, Ai Weiwei, Zhang Yonghe, Cui Kai, Alberto Kalach, Matti Sanaksenaho and Pirjo Sanaksenaho

Scale 1:7,000

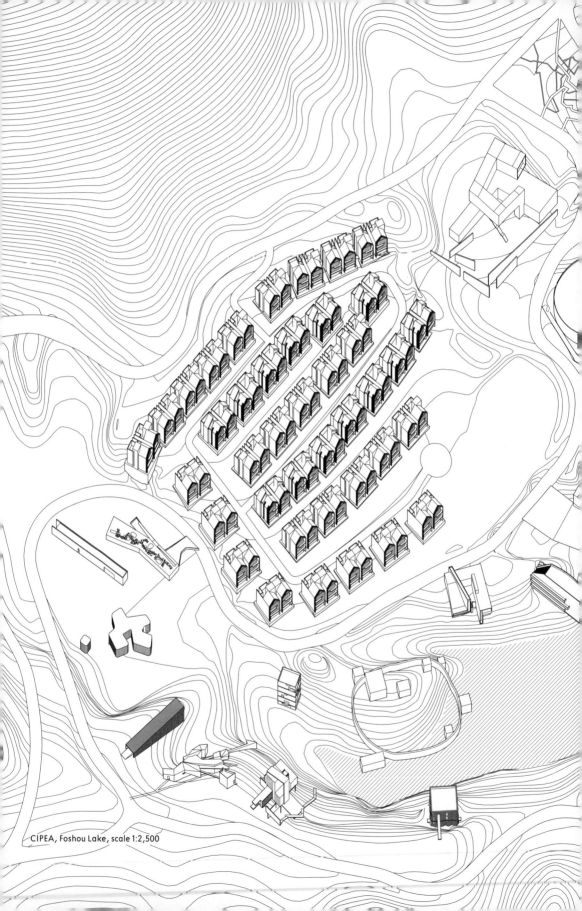

CIPEA, Foshou Lake, scale 1:2,500

1

2

3

1   Sifang Art Museum by Steven Holl
2   Interior view of the elevated gallery space
3   View up from the underground gallery space
4   The central courtyard of the museum

4

5

5   Hotel Monochrome by Liu Jiakun
6   Recreation Center by Ettore Sottsass
7   Inside the Conference Center by Arata Isozaki
8   View from Sifang Art Museum, overlooking the Conference
Center, with the Recreation Center to the left, and Hotel
Monochrome to the right

6

7

8

1

2

3

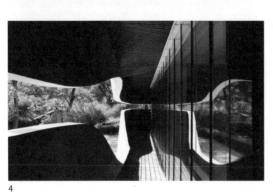

4

5

6

7

1   A Folded House by Doreen Heng Liu and the Boat House by
Matti Sanaksenaho and Pirjo Sanaksenaho seen from a distance
2   Inside the San-He Residence by Wang Shu
3   Fo-Shou House by Luis M. Mansilla and Emilio Tuñón
4   View into the loggia of the Block House by Zhang Lei
5   On the deck of the Waterside Pavilion by Alberto Kalach
6   Inside the Boat House by Matti Sanaksenaho and Pirjo
Sanaksenaho
7   Six Rooms by Ai Weiwei
8   View down onto the cascading passage along the facade of
the Shadows of Bamboo House by Sean Godsell

8

1

2

1   24 Cubes, the first residential development of Sunac's
Nanjing Peach Flower Garden
2   The second residential development of Nanjing Peach
Flower Garden

Right
View from the Pond Lily House by Mathias Klotz onto the villas
under construction of the second residential development

Shanghai   Pudong   Lujiazui

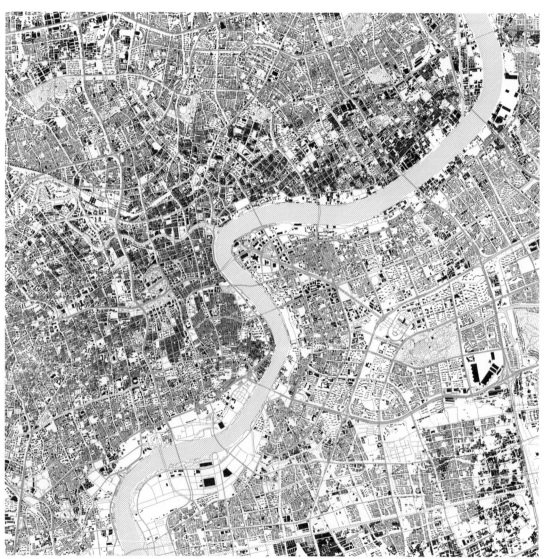

Central Shanghai, scale 1:100,000

Lujiazui:
The Added Value of Elevation

The normative morphological framework of a European and American city is proportional, but parts of cities often develop disproportionally, swelling up into enormous bulks. The cathedrals in European cities—Florence (figure 1), Cologne (figure 2), Salisbury (figure 3)—looming large in the horizon and overshadowing everything else, are elaborately decorated and disproportionally large rooms. They formed the center of Central Spiritual Districts, or CSDs, foretelling the arrival of the Central Business Districts, or CBDs, that began in American cities in Chicago and New York in the early twentieth century. Max Weber insisted that the spirit of capitalism is rooted in religion (albeit a particular school of religious following);[1] perhaps in bringing CSDs and CBDs in close parallel we seem to be grasping the material dimensions of Weber's claim. Instead of enormous rooms, we are now invested in very tall buildings.

The spirit of capitalism relied on dazzling visual effects, at a time aptly named as "the Gilded Age," with its thin veneer of ornamental richness stretched to the maximum to produce urban spectacles of CBDs. While the church could take land forcefully to build its large rooms, capitalism holds individual land ownership as one of its key moral cornerstones; it was left with no choice but to build tall. Time was right for tall buildings in the late nineteenth and early twentieth centuries when America invented the steel tube-frame and the electrically powered elevator. The "typical floor" became a key cost efficient real estate strategy. It made perfect sense for the first tall building constructed with steel frame and elevators to be a home insurance company in Chicago in 1884 (figure 4). In speed of construction and size, even though not in originality, the Empire State Building (figure 5) brought the Gilded Age to its height, as its last symbol (the market crashed before it opened in 1931). It was constructed in the record speed of 18 months. Unremarkable as a piece of architecture, it nevertheless had the bulk to claim a place in the city of New York, transforming an ordinary urban district to a desirable business destination.

It is the prospect of growth that powered the CSDs and CBDs, with their enormous sizes only held in check by gravity. Both religious faith (mission) and capital

Figure 1: View of Florence. Lucantonio degli Uberti, after Francesco Rosselli, ca. 1500–1510, woodcut, Staatliche Museen Berlin.

Figure 2: Cologne Cathedral, long elevation, drawing by Maximilian H. Fuchs, engraving by Christian Duttenhofer, in Boisserée's *Ansichten, Risse und einzelne Teile des Domes von Köln*, Stuttgart, 1823–31

Figure 3: John Constable, Salisbury Cathedral as seen from the Bishop's Grounds, c. 1825

Figure 4: Home Insurance Building, Chicago Illinois, 1931, Library of Congress, https://www.loc.gov/item/2014648256/

Figure 5: The Empire State Building, Lewis Wickes Hine, 1931, New York Public Library

(investment) are endless accumulations; both are in dire need for material demonstrations of their inherent truths.

CBDs, as symbols of capitalism, are far more successful globally than CSDs, even though they share an internal growth logic. The CBDs of Chicago and New York influenced the world with cities such as Toronto, Tokyo, Singapore, and Hong Kong attempting to create their own CBDs with similar architectural strategies; the central innovations of steel-frame construction and the elevator continued to be the anchoring elements for CBDs. Surprisingly, little changed since the early days of Chicago and New York. In this context, perhaps Shanghai's Lujiazui shifted CBDs in a different direction.

Lujiazui is the original CBD of China after it joined the World Trade Organization in 2001; from the very start, Lujiazui was different from its predecessors. Unlike Chicago and New York, Lujiazui has no land ownership limitation; the land for Lujiazui was freshly assembled from village farmlands across the Huangpu River from the city center of Shanghai. Despite the absence of one of the key forces behind the high-rise buildings of American CBDs, Lujiazui was purposefully planned as if it resulted from the limitation of land. It was constructed as if the skyline was its primary goal. Lujiazui was constructed "to be seen": either from across the Huangpu River on the Bund or from the top of its tall buildings. This understanding is substantiated by the simultaneous construction of a new, elevated promenade along the Bund for viewing Lujiazui. If the urban spectacles of Chicago and New York were incidental consequences of impatient capital working within the city to produce urban spectacles, Shanghai began with an urban spectacle and retrofitted it with a city.

The CBD in Shanghai was transformed from capitalistic incidents to a Chinese figure. As a figure, it contains many of its central features, most prominently through a catalog of excessively precious goods. Dominating the general scene is the heights of buildings, led by Shanghai Tower, followed by Oriental Pearl Tower, World Financial Center, and Jinmao Tower; the entourage of these is made of middling towers of middling architectural merits, forming the central urban mass of Lujiazui. Unlike Chicago and New York where the urban grids based on pedestrian and horse traffic remained intact, Lujiazui was entirely designed by the figure (tall buildings and a central Century Avenue), with the consideration of human movement as an afterthought. Central to Lujiazui is the elevated walkway system, highly contrived in a newly constructed CBD with no existing buildings and streets to navigate away from. The elevated walkway system of Lujiazui is the only way to walk in Lujiazui; in this status, it is a figure of elevated walkway with an exaggerated presence. If the skyline of Lujiazui was designed to be seen from the Bund, the height of the buildings are also designed for their viewing platforms, with the in-between spaces filled with offices and hotels. The Home Insurance Company building in Chicago did not conceive a viewing experience from the top of the building, and the viewing platform of the Empire State Building in New York consisted of nothing more than a roof area. The viewing platform—or viewing galleries—of the tallest buildings in Lujiazui are elaborate affairs, complete with thrills of digitally produced effects of crumbling structures, glass floors, gift shops, coffee shops, and souvenir photography. The lift technologies are remarkable; Shanghai Tower is fitted with the world's fastest elevator designed by Mitsubishi Electric and travelling at 20.5 meters (67 feet) per second. The commodities in the shopping malls in Lujiazui are largely high-end products, priced excessively at a level of symbolic conspicuous consumption. Lujiazui's urban hygiene is very elaborately maintained compared with many other Chinese cities where urban cleanliness presents a huge challenge; in Lujiazui, in stark contrast, teams of uniformed cleaners incessantly sweep and wipe all surfaces, matching the cleaners on gondolas for the tall buildings with vast areas of glass curtain walls. Young urban professionals are preciously dressed in their business suits, identification badges, professional leather briefcases, and expensive shoes. At times even the tourists are excessive in their unfiltered curiosity through their selfie sticks and cheerful holiday attires.

So outlandish is Lujiazui's walkway system that Hollywood made use of Lujiazui in its depiction of the future Los Angeles in Spike Jonze's 2013 movie *Her* (figure 6) in which the protagonist navigates on the elevated walkway surrounded by tall buildings on his way to work.

If the urban spectacles of Chicago and New York were incidental consequences of impatient capital working within the city to produce urban spectacles, Shanghai began with an urban spectacle and retrofitted it with a city.

CBDs in Chinese cities resemble a development model that is sometimes referred to as the developmental state.[2] Developmental state uses urbanization as an economic strategy to establish an investment and consumption cycle with real estate at the center of economic activities. It has proven to be enormously successful, sparking perhaps the most spectacular urban growth in China in the history of urbanization. China's urbanization rate increased from about 18 percent in 1978 to about 60 percent in 2018, an increase of urban population of about 659 million. Lujiazui is the visual symbol and the central figure of this massive migration of people and immense quantity of construction of buildings.

Figure 6: *Her*, directed by Spike Jonze, Annapurna Pictures / Warner Brothers, Sony Pictures, 2013

Lujiazui's influence is enormous; it established the Chinese model of figurative CBDs for all Chinese cities, which followed Shanghai's developmental path. Lujiazui may look like CBDs in other global cities, yet it has a very different logic and impact in China. All Chinese CBDs, such as those in Hangzhou, Suzhou, Guangzhou, are staged with enormous resources and astonishing architecture forming spectacles of skylines in measured distances away from the traditional city centers.

1

Max Weber, *The Protestant Ethic and the Spirit of Capitalism*, London and Boston: Unwin Hyman, 1905/1930.

2

You-tien Hsing, *The Great Urban Transformation, Politics of Land and Property in China*, Oxford: Oxford University Press, 2010.

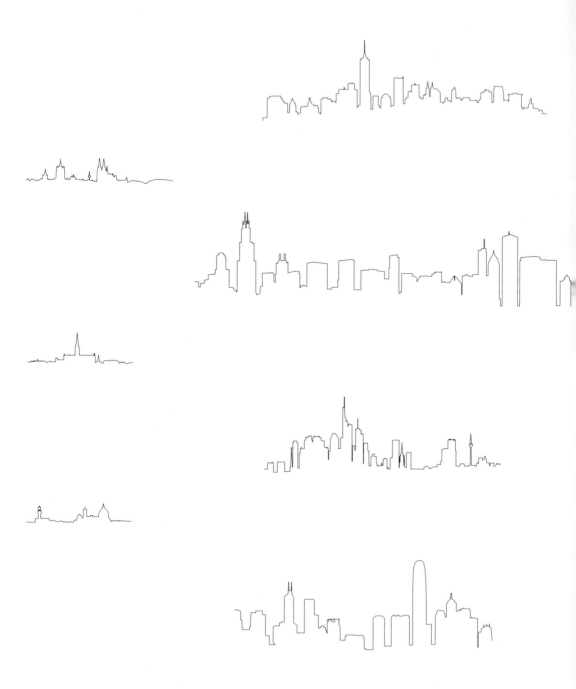

Central Spiritual District
Cologne, Salisbury, Florence

Central Business District
New York City, Chicago, Frankfurt, Hong Kong

The production of the skyline: religion, commerce, and spectacle

Central Business District as an Image
Shanghai, Suzhou, Hangzhou

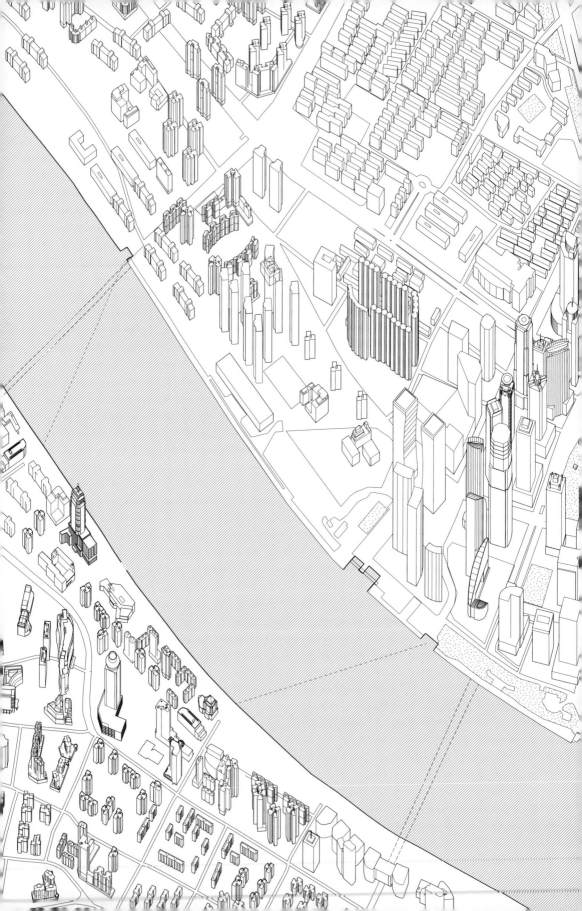

Lujiazui, scale 1:10,000

Ingredients for a Central Business District

As China's first central business district Lujiazui has had an enormous impact on the rise of central business districts in other Chinese cities. The success of Lujiazui is grounded in its careful curation of desirable components symbolizing China's modernity. All these components are explicitly and deliberately displayed in full view as functions and as spectacles.

View of Lujiazui toward Jinmao Tower and Oriental Pearl Tower
with the Bund seen in a distance on the opposite river bank

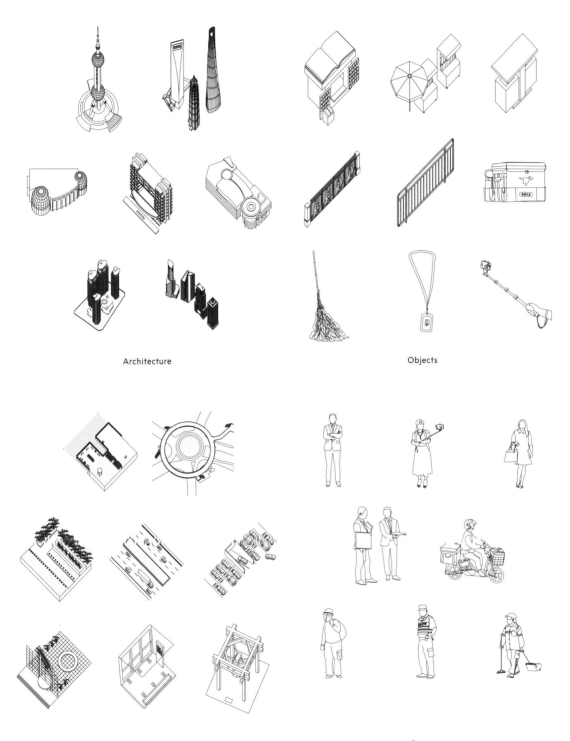

Architecture

Objects

Infrastructure

Persons

High Value Matrix

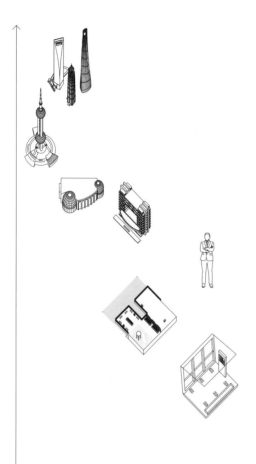

Expensive

Moderate

Inexpensive

Singular

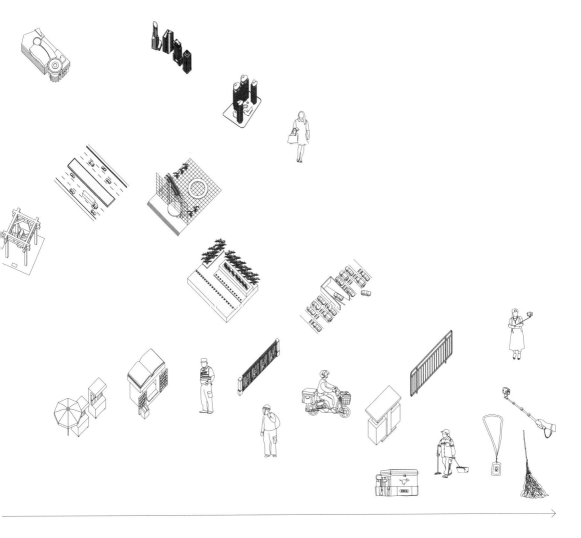

Multiple   Abundant

Architecture

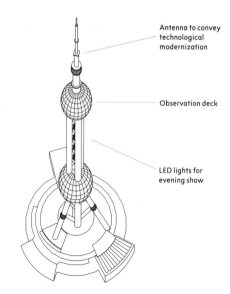

TV Tower

Built to transmit television signals, the tower is the earliest icon and tourist attraction of Lujiazui.

Antenna to convey technological modernization

Observation deck

LED lights for evening show

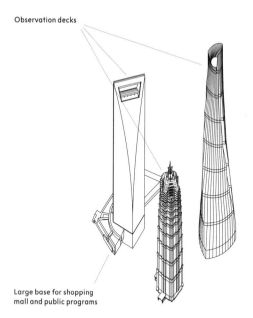

Observation decks

Large base for shopping mall and public programs

The Super Talls

Very tall buildings designed by the world's leading architectural firms project financial strength. Similarly programmed with observation decks, hotels, offices, and shopping malls, each building nevertheless presents a distinctive figure.

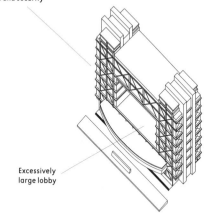

Oversized structural members to communicate strength and security

Excessively large lobby

Stock Exchange

Shaped like a gateway with oversized structural members and oversized lobby, this building functions and serves as the symbolic heart of China's financial capabilities.

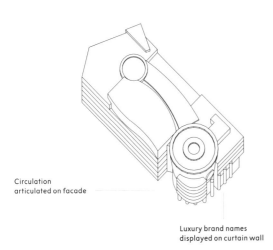

Circulation
articulated on facade

Luxury brand names
displayed on curtain wall

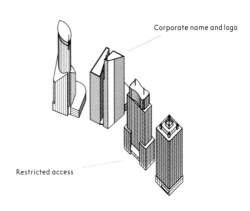

Corporate name and logo

Restricted access

Shopping Malls

Shopping malls encapsulate pedestrian movements which are separated from the vehicular movements through an extensive network of elevated platforms, maximizing their function as the center of social and commercial life in Lujiazui.

Office Towers

Lujiazui is also made of an ecosystem of aspiring office towers each striking a distinctive figure in bids to gain recognition in the skyline of Lujiazui.

Symbol of global
competitiveness

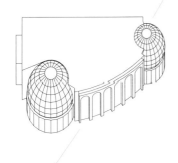

European classical
architectural elements
conveying sophistication

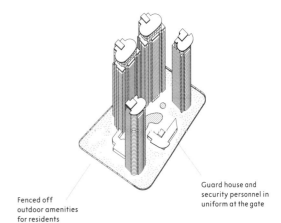

Fenced off
outdoor amenities
for residents

Guard house and
security personnel in
uniform at the gate

Convention Center

Flanking the European-style arcade applications are two enormous glass globes giving rise to the figure of rootedness of Shanghai's culture and its global aspirations.

Residential Towers

The real estate value of the residential units are protected by the proximity to the financial center, the fenced-off private amenities, and lightly themed architectural appearances.

Infrastructure

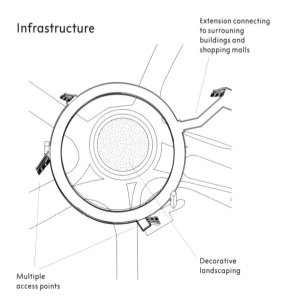

Extension connecting to surrouning buildings and shopping malls

Multiple access points

Decorative landscaping

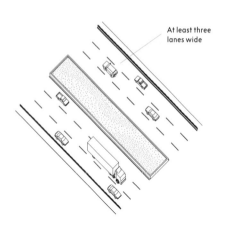

At least three lanes wide

Elevated Walkways

An extensive network of elevated walkways enhances the experiences of walking, shopping, and phototaking against the background of the tall buildings.

Highways

Designed to generate high-volume fast traffic with multiple lanes, bridges, and tunnels, Lujiazui's highways are an explicit demonstration of the automobile's articulation of the city in Lujiazui.

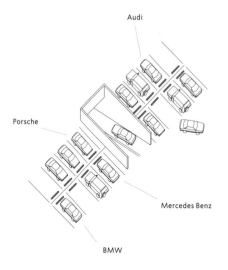

Audi

Porsche

Mercedes Benz

BMW

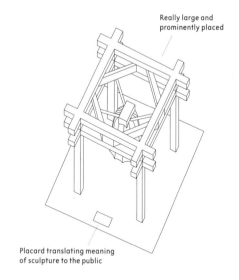

Really large and prominently placed

Placard translating meaning of sculpture to the public

Parking

Located either under buildings or alongside highways and streets, parking spaces are both functional and exhibitionist.

Public Art

Located at key intersections, public art pieces celebrate wealth and power, cultural sophistication, and the care of the municipal government and private developers for Lujiazui's public space.

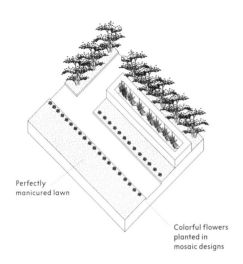

Perfectly
manicured lawn

Colorful flowers
planted in
mosaic designs

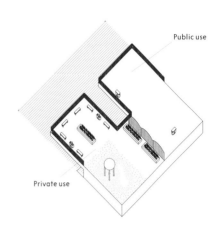

Public use

Private use

Urban Planting

Urban planting in Lujiazui focuses on the creation of color patterns and plant shapes for visual delight, heavily edged with hard construction materials. The hard edge also forms a barrier between the public and urban planting.

Waterfront

Lujiazui's waterfront is designed to protect people from water and to allow the viewing of Shanghai's central urban area across the river. The access to the water itself is entirely functional and kept to a minimum.

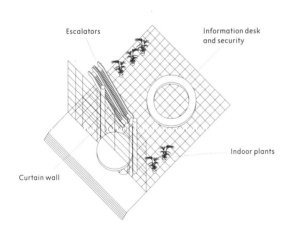

Escalators

Information desk
and security

Indoor plants

Curtain wall

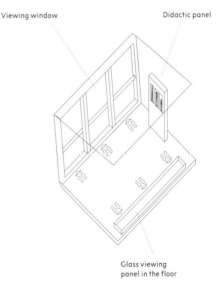

Viewing window

Didactic panel

Glass viewing
panel in the floor

Lobbies

Lobbies are highly articulated spaces in all buildings, serving both as triage and security as well as the face of the commercial operation.

Observation Decks

Shanghai's urban spectacle is embodied in the meticulous attention to the design of its observation decks on top of supertall buildings, underlying the centrality of vision for figuration.

Objects

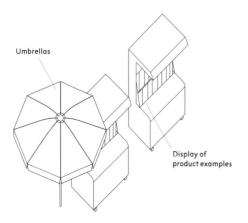

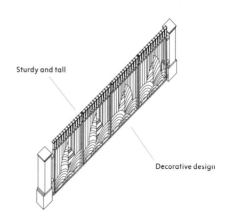

Kiosks

Kiosks mitigate the large scale of the elevated pedestrian walk-ways while providing photography services in desirable locations, augmenting the authority of the figure in Lujiazui's skyline.

Security Fences and Gates

Security and exclusivity are ensured by decorative fences and gates around residential and institutional compounds.

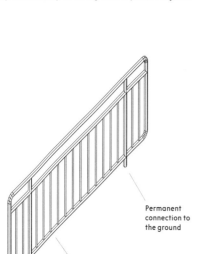

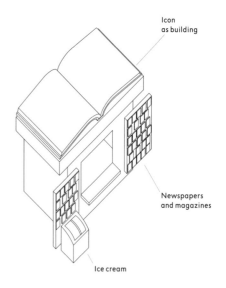

Crowd Control Barriers

Crowd control barriers ensure that vehicular and pedestrian movements are strictly separated.

Street Vendors

Street vendors fill in long pedestrian routes to provide temporary finer urban texture and basic food and beverage supplies.

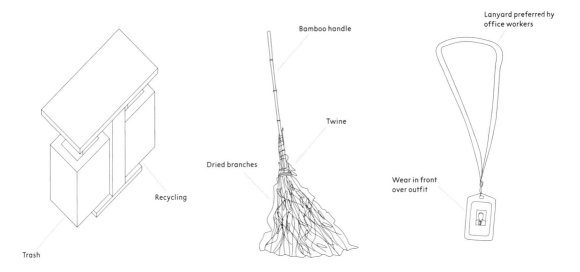

Bamboo handle

Lanyard preferred by
office workers

Twine

Dried branches

Wear in front
over outfit

Recycling

Trash

Trash Bins

Trash Bins are placed very close to one
another to highlight the importance of dis-
posing waste in controlled manner.

Brooms

Brooms made from bamboo symbolize
the act of manual cleaning of streets.
The corporeal dedication highlights the
importance of urban hygiene in Lujiazui.

Badges

Ostensibly, badges are used for
identification in offices, they are also
explicit markings of legitimacy and status.

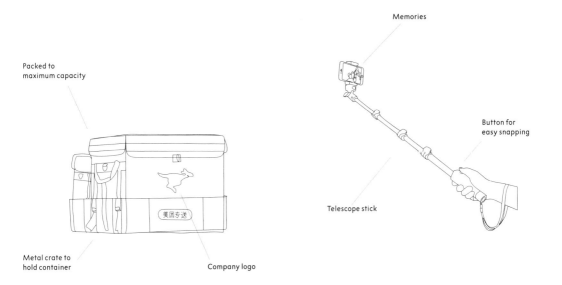

Memories

Packed to
maximum capacity

Button for
easy snapping

Telescope stick

Metal crate to
hold container

Company logo

Delivery Containers

Delivery containers and scooters transformed express courier
services in China, making the delivery of daily lunches for office
workers an affordable and viable business.

Selfie Stick

Selfie sticks turned the making of selfies from a casual action
to a dedicated one, something that found exceptional cultural
empathy in China.

Persons

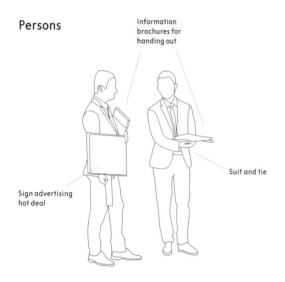

Information
brochures for
handing out

Suit and tie

Sign advertising
hot deal

Branded handbag

Folders

Not her commuter
shoes

Real Estate Agents

Real estate agents persistently pursue visitors, offering the materialization of living in an urban spectacle for a very high price. They can be found at their agencies, at the entrances of shopping malls, and directly in front of the properties for sale.

Investment Bankers

There is a large concentration of national and international investment banks that view Shanghai as both an investment opportunity and a location of prestige.

Took countless photos
on her phone today

Cell phone

Selfie stick

Tourists

Mostly domestic tourists come to Lujiazui as one of the "must-see" sights in Shanghai. Primed via the tourist tunnel as the arrival route to Lujiazui, visitors are engaged by spectacles, shopping, and entertainment throughout the day.

Developers

Some developers have their offices located in the office towers in Lujiazui.

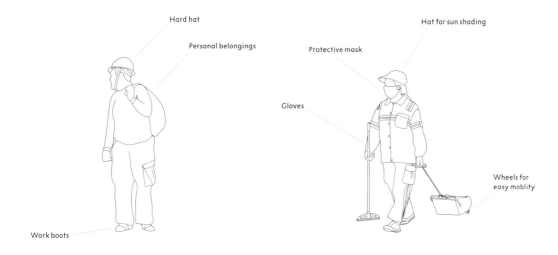

Hard hat

Personal belongings

Hat for sun shading

Protective mask

Gloves

Work boots

Wheels for easy moblity

Construction Workers

Construction workers are often housed on site to avoid wasteful daily journeys and to increase the speed of construction.

Street Cleaners

Generously deployed street cleaners sweep Lujiazui incessantly, and at the same time they display the act of cleaning the city with their elaborate uniform and equipment.

Delivery boxes

Helmet with shield

Electric scooter

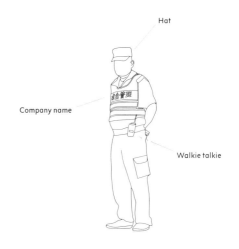

Hat

Company name

Walkie talkie

Delivery Persons

The Chinese labor force operates at a manual, personal, and flexible scale, giving rise to individual franchises of delivering services.

Security Guards

Dressed to be seen with authority, security guards are a welcome presence in which peace of life in cities is grounded.

Office Buildings

Office buildings are the neutral tone against which strongly figurated buildings—the Oriental Pearl Tower, Jinmao Tower, World Trade Center, and Shanghai Tower—distinguish them-selves as highlights. This parallels the financial neutral tone embodied in these office buildings for global financial corporations.

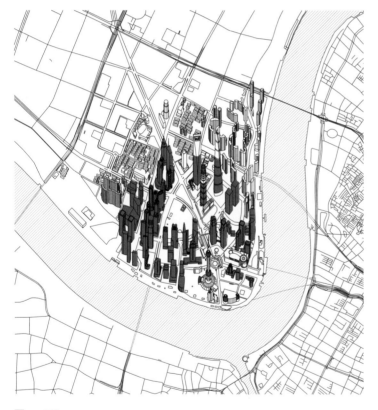

■ Offices

Right
Shanghai Stock Exchange, scale 1:1,000

1

2

1   Office buildings surrounding the central area of Lujiazui
2   Two office workers taking a smoke on the elevated walkway
3   View from the elevated walkway toward the Hong Kong
invested International Finance Center podium and shopping mall
4   Public Art of rings on the steps of the New Shanghai
International Tower
5   Office workers having lunch in the canteen of Taiping
Finance Tower
6   Shanghai Stock Exchange Building
7   A street cleaner

3

4

5

6

7

Gated Residential Developments

Highrise gated residential developments next to the
office buildings in Lujiazui offer the ultimate fulfillment of
aspirations to prosperity, accomplishment, and security,
unimaginable just decades ago. For most residents, the
status symbol more than compensates the inconvenience of
daily life due to its remoteness to Shanhai's urban centers.

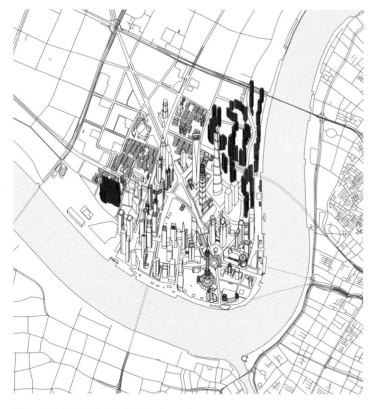

■ Gated Private Residential Developments
▨ Government Subsidized Housing

Right
Residential Area along Huangpu River, scale 1:3,500

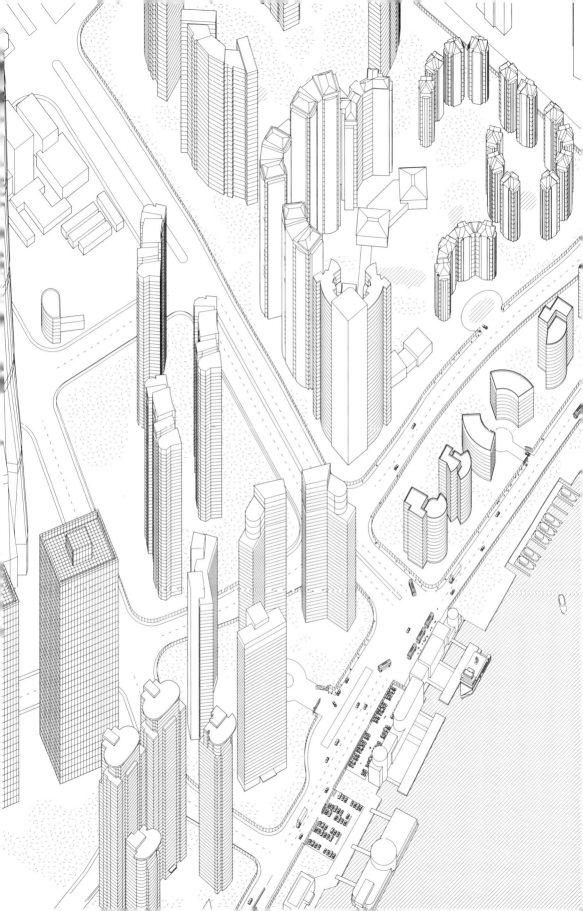

1

2

3

4

5

1   Private residential development at Alley 99 Shangcheng Road
2   The gate to the private residential development No. 1
Ocean View
3   A window display of a real estate agent's office
4   Private residential development Yanlord Garden
5   Real estate agents waiting for potential buyers in front of
Yanlord Garden
6   School bus for the Wellington College International, Shanghai

6

7

9

10

8

11

7   Gate to the residential community Number Four Dongyuan
New Village, built in the 1980s as a government-subsidized
residential area with public amenities
8   Bird's-eye view of Dongchang New Village and Dongyuan
New Village
9   The security guard at the gate of Number Four Dongyuan
New Village
10   A market inside Dongyuan New Village
11   Residences inside Dongyuan New Village
12   A schoolgirl doing homework at a restaurant inside Dongyuan
New Village

12

Tourism

The conspicuous display of valuable things and the provision
of viewing infrastructure draw a large number of sight-seers.
The formal character of Lujiazui and the spectacle-enchanted
tourists produce one another through a symbiotic relationship.

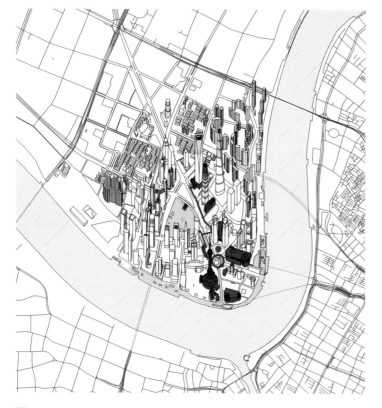

■ Main Tourism/Shopping Artery

▨ Secondary Tourist Areas (Hotel, Parks Waterfront, etc.)

Right
Elevated Walkway and Superbrand Mall, scale 1:250

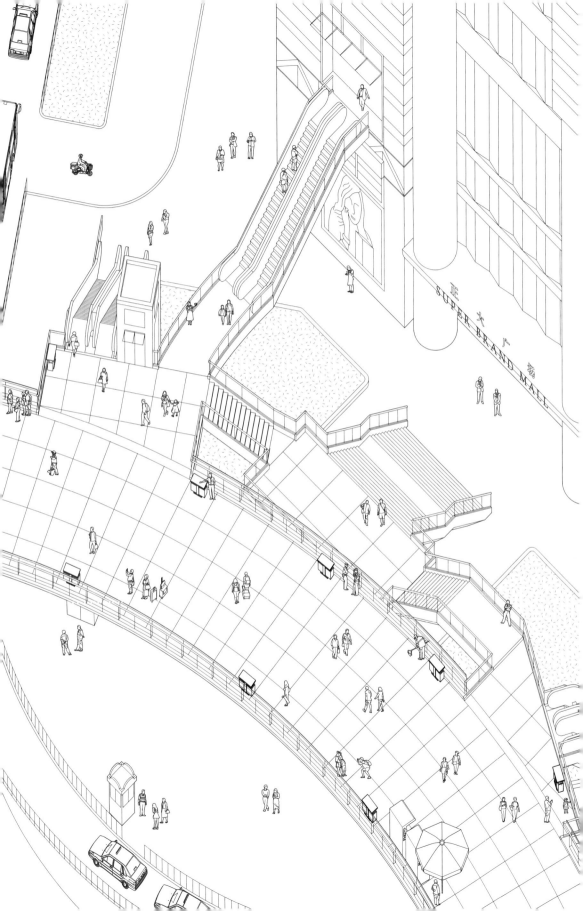

1

2

3

4

5

6

8

7

1   A ride in the tourist tunnel from the Bund to Lujiazui
2   Disney's flagship store in Lujiazui
3   Access to the circular elevated walkway
4   A family photo
5   Photography kiosks
6   View onto the circular elevated walkway
7   Interior view of the Superbrand Mall
8   The three Super Talls in Lujiazui: the World Trade Center,
Jinmao Tower, and Shanghai Tower
9   A group of tourists on the glass-bottomed skywalk at
Jinmao Tower

9

Shanghai   Pudong   Nanhui New Town

Nanhui New Town, scale 1:100,000

Nanhui New City:
The Oversized Circle

Oversized circle as a city plan has many historical precedents; Nanhui New City (formerly known as Lingang New City), despite the resemblance to other precedents, emerges from a Chinese imagination of figuration, which perhaps accounts for its confidence in letting the oversized circle run its logical course in the design of the city.

While the New World loves the grid, the European Enlightenment flirted with the oversized circle, which had already been explored in the Renaissance through the "centralized design" such as that which shaped Palmanova (figure 1). The functions of the city perhaps struggle most violently with the oversized circle, yet the centralized design continuously stakes its boldness in defiance. The Enlightenment mind and the Revolutionary spirit of France in the eighteenth century inspired a new era of fascination with the oversized circle. Unable to realize an oversized circle in a factory project for the Royal Saltworks, Ledoux brought it to its intended goal in a publication, calling it the "ideal city of Chaux" (figure 2) in 1804. Ledoux's modern modular rhapsody of Italian classicism, in this ideal city, submits to the dictation of the circular plan, which in turn gives rise to the collaborative architectural forms of the rest of the city.

Figure 1: Plan of Palmanova, Italy, engraving by Frans Hogenberg, 1598, Rijksmuseum Amsterdam

The center of the oversized circle, in this case, marks a distinctive feature of the European (or Indo-European) spatial imagination. Like its ancient precedent of the Round City of Baghdad (762–766), Ledoux's Chaux creates a central authority often underlined architecturally in the grand projects of the *Ancien Régime*, which ascends to a spiritual level through religious canons or republican ideals. Ledoux argued that "everything is circular in nature": ripples, planetary motion, ocean currents, rehearsing a "natural religion" that reconstituted the idealistic imaginations of the divine perfection of the circular form. The ideal city of Chaux remains a drawing, so as many city designs based on the idea of the oversized circle. Perhaps the oppressive nature of the oversized circle, despite the perfection of the form, has been too costly functionally and intellectually, credible only as an ideal diagram not be taken too literally like Ebenezer Howard's Garden City. Until, that is, Nanhui New City made its appearance.

Figure 2: Bird's-eye view of the Ideal City of Chaux by Nicholas Ledoux, engraving, 1804

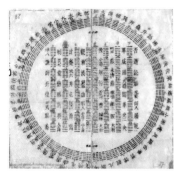

Figure 3: Diagram of *I Ching* hexagrams owned by Gottfried Wilhelm Leibnitz, 1701, author unknown, Leibnitz Archive, Niedersächsische Landesbibliothek

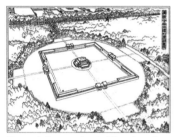

Figure 4: A reconstructed drawing of a Han dynasty (202 BCE to 9 CE) ritual complex in Xi'an. From *Zhongguo Gudai Jianzhushi*, Beijing, 1980, p.47

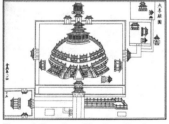

Figure 5: Drawing of Daxiangdian in *Da Ming Huidian* (1587); the building is now known as Qiniandian, or the Hall of Prayer for Good Harvests

What does Nanhui New City possess that gives it immunity to functional and intellectual anxieties associated with the oversized circle in the European and American contexts? Nanhui New City's existence may have resulted from an understanding of the oversized circle as the shape of heaven in a "round heaven and square earth" narrative (figure 3). Heaven (*tian*) here is not connected with the religious notion of heaven in Indo-European cultures; it is, on the contrary, a conception of one of the two basic cosmological elements: the solid ground and the fluid sky. The fluid sky is understood as being round: an oversized circle. This idea goes much deeper than a morphological understanding of the universe; it is intertwined with the *yin-yang* conception of all things, the idea that each thing is tethered with its opposite in simultaneous contrast and harmony. Heaven and earth, it would seem, is the very first *yin-yang* pair, and it is invested with enormous amount of study over its long history from the time of the *Book of Changes* in ninth century BCE. Early Chinese architecture and planning made use of this principle, such as an important ritual complex in the dynasty of West Han (205 BCE to 9 CE) called Mingtang Piyong (figure 4). The circular-square combination has been brought into many realizations, particularly with projects of high cultural prestige, such as Beijing's Temple of Heaven (figure 5) and the stadium and swimming complex for the 2008 Beijing Olympic Games. The Chinese circular-square duo is very different from the triad of the Indo-European dialectic; the dialectic introduces a third element of "synthesis" while stressing the struggle of thesis and antithesis. While the oversized circle would not survive the thesis and antithesis struggle, it can clearly do much better in the *yin-yang* schema.

Before Nanhui New City took shape, the oversized circle featured prominently in Shanghai's aspiration; it witnessed a scheme symbolic of Shanghai's rise, the master plan of Pudong by Richard Rogers between 1992 and 1994 (figure 6), a much favored scheme of an invited international competition.[1] Here, Rogers proposed an oversized circle with a park in the center, which left a deep impression for Shanghai's aspiring planners. Although a more balanced scheme from Chinese planners was eventually adopted, the oversized circle was kept alive and found another life in Nanhui New City.

Nanhui New City owes its existence to an ambitious master plan after the development of Pudong, the

Shanghai Master Plan 2001–2020, which first realized
the idea of urbanization as the key strategy of national
economic development, heralding decades of new city creation in all parts of China. This Master Plan took the lead
to create "new cities" of many varieties, serving as a giant
laboratory of Chinese urbanization. China's membership
of the World Trade Organization in 2001 was perhaps a key
factor in Shanghai's grand ambitions; from 2001 to 2010,
Shanghai's population grew from 6.62 million to 23 million.[2] This is a case of the "build new cities and people
will come" approach. Shanghai's strategy has been "one
central city, nine new cities, sixty small towns, and six
hundred villages" (1-9-6-6); Nanhui New City is one of the
nine new cities, with a distinctive character.

Meinhard von Gerkan of gmp, the Hamburg-based
architectural firm that master planned the new city,
spoke of Nanhui New City as having "no context," meaning no "human context"; this "lack of context" justified
the imposition of an oversized circular design. Unlike
other new cities in Shanghai that relied on the creation
of new and exotic cultural identities, Nanhui New City
is a bold move toward the future. Its oversized circle is

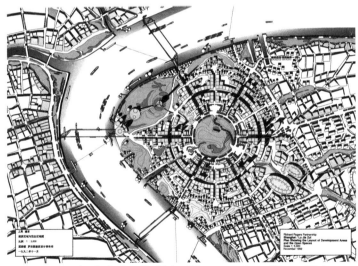

Figure 6: Master plan for Lujiazui by Richard Rogers, courtesy of Rogers Stirk
Harbour + Partners

While the oversized circle would not survive the thesis
and antithesis struggle, it can clearly do much better in
the *yin-yang* schema.

centered with a lake of 2.5 kilometers in diameter, poetically named the "water drop" (*dishui*). From the lake, bands of commercial, greenery, and residential zones ripple into ever-larger circles making up an area of 315 square kilometers, demanding more and more functional areas for the city (figure 7). It is projected to have a population of 800,000, although a quarter of that number lived in Nanhui New City in 2018.[3] The new city is governed by a development authority, which delegates actual developments to

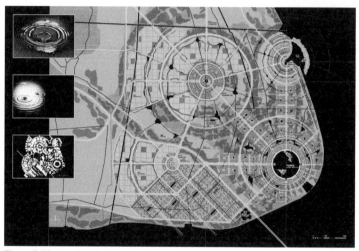

Figure 7: Master plan for Lingang New City (Nanhui New Town) by Gerkan, Marg and Partners Architects (gmp), courtesy of gmp Architects

eight corporations, each responsible for one section of the city. Nanhui's main economic rationale is its closeness to the Pudong International Airport and its container port; it is now able to include Tesla's gigafactory and many off-campus facilities of the universities in Shanghai. This economic strategy anchors real estate developments and competes with the central city of Shanghai with lower prices, convenient transportation, and the luxury of a lake-front promenade and lake-front property.

The apparent paradox of European designers providing Shanghai with its most outstanding figuration is less problematic than it first appears. Shanghai, from its inception as an amalgamation of foreign concessions from 1840s, has held onto its tradition of internationalism. The "Chinese Shanghai" from the 1950s is fundamentally different from the "concession Shanghai" in the 1840s; while the Bund replicated the European waterfront city, the 1-9-6-6 plan is a Shanghai invention. Shanghai's aspiration to internationalism, as a Chinese city, is a complex, layered condition that is skillfully managed by foreign architects producing figuration for Chinese moral and aesthetic sensibilities.

1
Charlie Q. L. Xue, Hailin Shai, Brian Mitchenere, "Shaping Lujiazui: The Formation and Building of the CBD in Pudong, Shanghai," *Journal of Urban Planning* 16: 2, 209–32.
2
Jinghuan He, "Implementation of the Shanghai Master Plan (2001–2020)," paper presented to *AESOP 26th Annual Congress*, 2012, Ankara.
3
Zheng Wang, https://urban-china.org/governing-the-future-city/

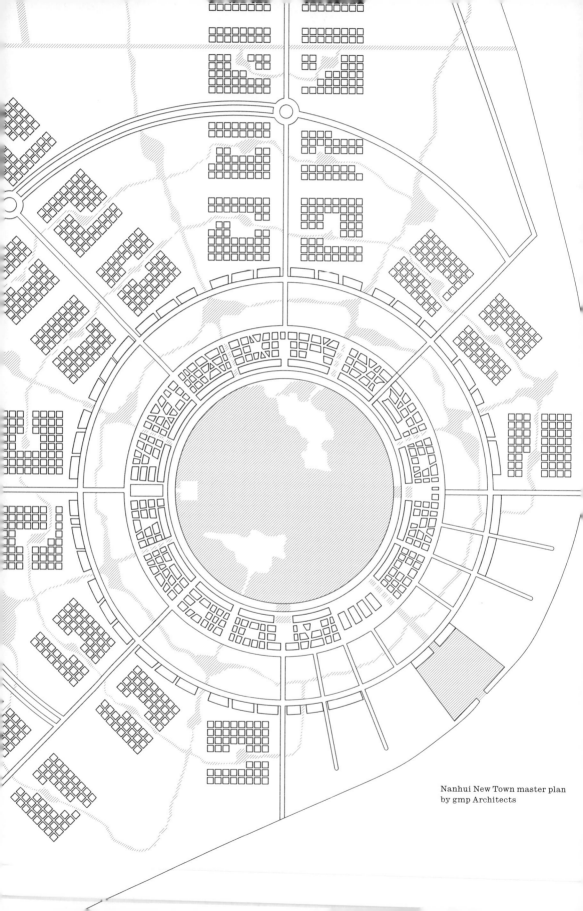

Nanhui New Town master plan
by gmp Architects

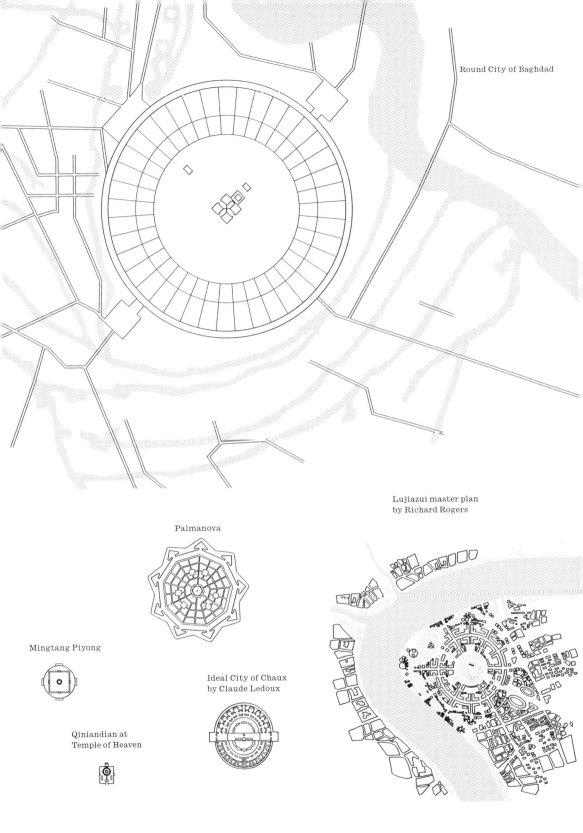

Round City of Baghdad

Lujiazui master plan
by Richard Rogers

Palmanova

Mingtang Piyong

Ideal City of Chaux
by Claude Ledoux

Qiniandian at
Temple of Heaven

The circle as the city and its increase in size
Scale 1:40,000

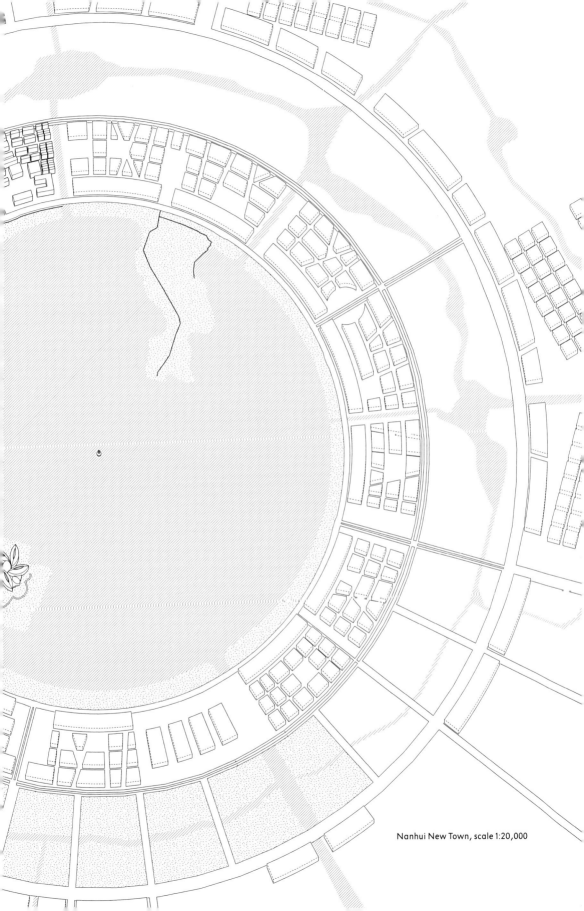

Nanhui New Town, scale 1:20,000

1

2

3

1 Sunken entrance plaza of Dishui Lake metro station
2 Office developments next to Dishui Lake metro station
3 Pedestrian crossing with electronic monitoring equipment
4 Bike and pedestrian paths along the waterfront
5 A loudspeaker on the lawn of the waterfront park
6 Newly landscaped waterfront park
7 A designated waterfront barbecue area on the West Island of Dishui Lake
8 Ticket office for boating
9 Waterfront promenade

4

5

6

7

8

9

Drift Trigger Three:

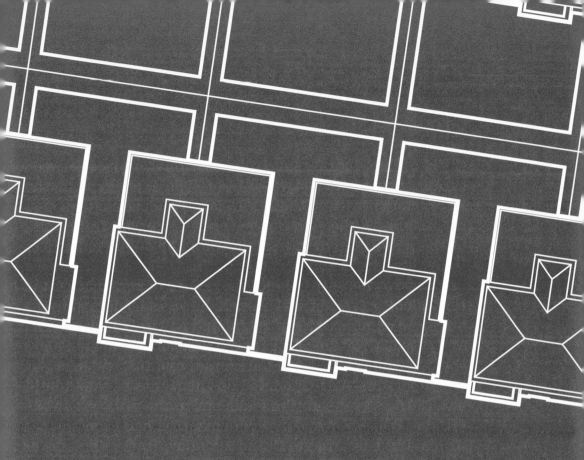

Group
Action

Group Action

Cities are not indifferent to civilizational choices between group action and individualism. The archetype of the European villa—and the single-family house as its democratization—is the defining feature of an urban framework of the public and private dichotomy. An entire culture of individualism is constructed on this first foundation: the exclusive ownership of land, the realms of personality and that of collective action through union and federation, the sizes and complexities of social and political institutions, and personalization of means of transport are shaping how the city should be. Even businesses and institutions—as "legal persons"—are modeled on the rights of the individual. China's group action leads not to the villa but to the village. While European modernization has been the act of leaving the village, China's modernization has never abandoned the village as its embryonic social and architectural form. The architectural and urban manifestations of Confucius's Great Sameness seem to be derivatives of the village: the work unit (*danwei*) and the residential community (*xiaoqu*) are contemporary versions of spaces designed for larger units of action. Within the spaces of these units, individual preferences in architecture are symbolic pledges of allegiance to the ability to act in unison for speed and impact. Group action, in this sense, remains one of the most powerful triggers of typological drift.

Jiepai New Village is how group action shapes the transformation of China's villages—by many measures a typical case study—as they transition from being rural to being urban. Jiepai New Village was formed through the merging of many "natural villages" to create larger agricultural fields and to establish village industries. Globalization demanded larger scales of production; these villages responded to the demands of globalization in radical ways. Invariably, in imagining their brave new future villages, it was the urban dwelling form that became their main inspiration; Jiepai New Village, instead of reinventing the architecture of traditional clustering of village houses, invited an urban-based architectural firm to provide a master plan, and chose to represent their new village through a gigantic flower pattern. By far the most astonishing example of group action is Huaxi Village, a spectacular assembly of skyscraper, pagoda-looking village administrative buildings, European-looking houses, and uniform rectangular housing blocks linked by a system of decorated walkways reminiscent of Beijing's imperial gardens. Huaxi Village is the epitome of group action in China's villages; it never abandoned collective ownership of land and property, and insists on strong family style leadership that strategizes the village economy as a whole within the larger marketplace of China and the world. Huaxi Village keeps its amalgamated agricultural land, operates a range of village industries, and runs a Village Capital investment firm that advertises itself on the screens of Times Square, New York. Despite its peculiar choices of architectural styles, Huaxi Village demonstrates a total and viable social, cultural, and economic fact: a version of the village-turned-city rooted in Chinese popular culture, pursuing its architectural goals almost unchecked by the mainstream tastes of urban planning authorities. Despite its architectural idiosyncrasies, Huaxi Village vividly illustrates the urban aspirations of the Great Sameness; could Huaxi Village as a model be reworked through an architecture of sophistication?

Distant derivatives of the village archetype in the past decade are China's university cities. Although they may be understood to have emerged from the economic and urban principle of "clustering"—similar perhaps to the clustering of research and production in Silicon Valley and at Stanford University, they are perhaps better framed as China's new technological villages testing a spatial form. China's university cities are not "organically grown" from economic demands of the marketplace, but are a state and municipal creation intending to accelerate the production of knowledge. They suggest the spatialization of "the group intellect" unimaginable in an individualistic culture. Refraining from immediate moralization and judgement, we should perhaps understand China's university cities as attempts to leverage on larger units of accountability and action in knowledge production. University cities appeared in China within a relatively short time span from the 2000s to 2010s, and they seem to have reached a saturation point today. University cities may be a result of the increasing pressure of rapid increase of university enrollment and municipal ambition to occupy more territories at the time. They may also indicate something far more fundamental: the future of higher education in China. China shares neither the history of medieval guilds in the form of *universitas*, nor the private sponsorship that characterizes the global university in the United States. Its traditional ideal form of knowledge production seems to be embedded in the institutional imagination of the advancement of the scholar, through centrally managed examinations and selections, from talent to central administration. University cities, not unlike the ancient infrastructure of imperial civil service examinations, could indeed capture this great state enterprise of education that would enable China to operate at the cutting edge of knowledge and innovation in the future.

Group action is not a herd mentality understood as an aberration of a preferred form of individual determination; it is a deliberate cultural and economic strategy deeply invested in the competitive advantage of its choices. In this context, the loss of individual agency is certainly real, but it must be understood in the context of greater sense of security, faster rates of production, a more coordinated platform for innovation, and higher quality shared infra-structure; all these are internalized as a preferred political and social form, and all these are sublimated as moral and aesthetic experiences. It is from this standpoint that the proponents of group action argue for its virtue, and the city becomes a product and a producer of the larger units of accountability and action.

Jiangsu Province

Zhenjiang

Jiepaizhen

Jiepai New Village and its environs, scale 1:100,000

Jiepai New Village: Harvesting Group Enlargement

Jiepai New Village is located next to Jiepai Town with a population of 50,000; it was created in 2006 by merging some 178 "natural villages" (14,500 peasants) to form a "super village" on a site of 100 hectares. This was largely the work of the city of Danyang, a provincial city in Jiangsu Province with its urban center some 30 kilometers away from Jiepai Town. Jiangsu has some of China's most fertile land due to its mild weather and abundant rainfall ideal for rice crop; for thousands of years, the land has been intensely cultivated. The "natural village" in this area is typically formed by unremarkable strips of two-story farm houses sandwiched between roads, irrigation canals, and private vegetable patches, surrounded by rice paddies (figure 1).

Figure 1: Strip villages of Danyang, Google Earth, Maxar Technologies, 2020

Guided by a series of central government policies that encouraged concentration of population and improvement of land-use efficiency, the city of Danyang pushed for this merge. China had about 4.2 million "natural villages" in 1990 (with an urbanization rate of 26 percent); this was reduced to about 2.8 million in 2013 (with an urbanization rate of 54 percent). This translates to the availability of 335,908 square kilometers of agricultural land for urban use, and 127 million peasants becoming a kind of urban dwellers. The parallel of this "primitive accumulation" to that of the Enclosure Movement in the early stages of capitalism in Europe is hard to miss; only in China it is larger in scale and faster in speed.[1] Shanghai led this dramatic transformation, inventing its "three concentrations" in

1985: the concentration of agricultural land to those with effective agricultural capabilities, the concentration of industrial facilities to industrial zones, and the concentration of dispersed rural population to townships. Jiepai New Village is a poster child of this "concentration" in material terms.

The creation of Jiepai New Village made available 26.3 square kilometers of land for urban and industrial use while slightly increasing land for agriculture resulting from improvement of land use efficiency. Jiepai New Village contains 6,400 households, over 300 villas, a community service center, schools, hospitals, and other forms of infrastructure, all costing 3.75 billion rmb.[2] The industrial production of Jiepai Town is deeply intertwined with that of Danyang City. Danyang now has a population of 981,600 with strong manufacturing capacities in auto parts, machine tools, lenses, wood furniture, and textiles. It is ranked 12th in China's most competitive counties in 2018. Both Danyang and the surrounding villages contributed and profited from Danyang's rise to prosperity; they have become joint stock holders of all new industries—focusing

Figure 2: A rendering of the Danyang International Auto City

on new technological capacities of manufacturing and high-value and large-scale agriculture—that have been enabled by the newly created urban land. The Danyang International Auto City, a one-stop shopping center for auto parts on a site of 80 hectares and 1.2 million square meters of space, is being constructed just next to Jiepai New Village (figure 2); this will make Jiepai New Village enormously attractive not just as center of labor and enterprises, but also in the real estate market. Jiepai New Village collaborated with the Danyang government in the lucrative real estate developments; it consists of residential units for peasants, which usually means non-commercial status without permits of resale, and residential units for sale with permits made available from the city of Danyang.

A change of this order of magnitude is a massive shock to all aspects of Chinese peasant life. While popular media tend to focus on dramatic resistance (as in the cases of dramatic holdouts known as "nail households," most of whom demanded more compensation rather than a return to rural life), the vast majority of peasants embraced the move. For them, the toil of rural life is hard to endure and the comfort of urban life is difficult to resist; this is in fact a familiar rags-to-riches story for the Chinese countryside. Jiepai New Village, with the provision of sewage, paved roads, parks, schools, kindergartens, hospitals, and entertainment and shopping facilities, is a great leap forward in standards of living; this immense upgrade clearly mitigated the enormous shock of change.

Figure 3: Leaflet advertising the Windsor Villa real estate development in Jiepai New Village

Perhaps the architecture of Jiepai New Village demonstrates this shock of change in the most vivid detail: a Chinese rural version of the *nouveaux riches* of the Gilded Age. With Shanghai's sensational Thames Town recently completed, Jiepai New Village's architecture followed a similar vein with some help from Shanghai's Tongji Architectural Design Group; Thames Town's English houses—and the perceived refinement of English gentility—became perhaps for Jiepai New Village the aspiration of the day (figure 3). At the center of Jiepai New Village are waterfront villas roughly following an English vernacular, surrounding an inner area of multi-story residential units, outlined by high-rise apartment blocks. On the other hand, traditional Chinese spatial imagination also came into play; the master plan is shaped like an eight-petaled flower surrounded by an artificial lake. Three Chinese traditional bridges are built across the artificial lake, the central bridge has nine "moon gate" arches, and two side bridges have three arches. The arched bridge—particularly those with nine arches—is a highly popular architectural feature invoking extensive poetic experiences in both literati

Perhaps the architecture of Jiepai New Village demonstrates this shock of change in the most vivid detail: a Chinese rural version of the *nouveaux riches* of the Gilded Age.

literature and popular culture, with iconic romantic tales taking place around arched bridges.

Neither Chinese *literati's* cultural sophistication nor the English gentry's *bourgeois* manners and estate offer spaces for the customs of peasant life, even as the villagers of Jiepai New Village appear to have adopted an urban architecture. Vertical living in high-rise buildings is alienating for peasants whose lives had so far been built around large ground-floor living rooms with open access to front yards. To compensate for this loss, many villagers converted their ground-floor garages into rural living spaces by placing sofas, benches, and entertainment facilities for card and chess games. For peasants, landscape is an urban taste too wasteful of land to contemplate; many Jiepai New Village residents removed ornamental plants and grass, and planted vegetables and herbs instead. Some still wash vegetables in the lake, and others dry foods on flat hard surfaces meant to be architectural and landscape features. The spatial practices of everyday peasant life are fighting back against urban architecture. Even though Jiepai New Village is a product of the logic of group action, all these details of spatial practice may be symptomatic of a terribly misconceived architecture.

Jiepai New Village seems to invite comparisons with versions of ideal living communities such as Palmanova as the Renaissance geometrical perfection, Savannah as the utilitarian English colonial enclave, Welwyn Garden City as idyllic English village life, Celebration as conspicuous American social privilege. None of these could sufficiently explain and contextualize Jiepai New Village. The conceptual framework of Jiepai New Village is neither religious nor intellectual; it was quite closely mapped on to the material organizations of villagers, manifested, like in numerous other new village developments in China, as a collection of desirable and precious objects. The speed and thoroughness of transformation are a testament to the social form of group action. The misfit of its architecture and the underlying lifeform is clear evidence that there is a long way to go to establish an architecture that serves all these demands in appropriate ways. Jiepai New Village is an example of the best of the type; it affirms an indisputable cultural logic in the pursuit of happiness in the Chinese countryside and highlights its architectural contradictions. It has the work cut out for Chinese architects whose attention, regrettably, has so far turned to elsewhere.

1

Zhang Yulin, "Understanding China's Enclosures," *Chinese Village Discovery (Zhongguo xiangcun faxian)* 3, 2014; "The Great Clearance: A Comparison of the Enclosure Movements in China and United Kingdom," *Journal of China University of Agriculture (Zhongguo nongye daxue xuebao)* 1, 2015, pp.19–45.

2

Reported in China Daily on December 31, 2015. http://www.chinadaily.com.cn/trending/2015-12/31/content_22885090_2.htm.

The Natural Village

Before and after: from natural villages to the new village
Scale 1:40,000

The New Village

Jiepai New Village, scale 1:10,000

1

3

2

1   British-style row houses around a church that serves as the
management and sales office
2   One of the residential streets lined by row houses
3   Looking past the highrise housing for relocated villagers
toward the real estate development
4   Looking across the water toward the new villagers housing

4

5

6

7

8

5   The central bridge in traditional style with nine
moongate arches
6   Villagers housing with ground-floor commercial
spaces upon completion of construction
7   One of the entrance gates to Jiepai New Village
8   New villagers housing

1   A British-style house converted to an Italian-style
villa with multiple additional spaces added
2   A vegetable growing area on the roof
3   Elderly villagers socializing on the street
4   Vegetable growing area and laundry lines in the
community garden

5 A villager washing reed leaves in ornamental water body
6 A garage converted into a sitting area
7 A villager drying beans in the communal outdoor space
8 Villagers engaged in "square dance" in the communal
outdoor space

5

6

7

8

Jiangsu Province

Wuxi

Huaxicun

Huaxi Village and its environs, scale 1:100,000

Huaxi Village:
The Rural Chinese Dream

Huaxi's interpretation of the Great Sameness (*datong*) is literal; it has meant uniform and disciplined life with hierarchy in return for the security of a safety net. This, on the other hand, has been a common political ideal in rural China of which Huaxi is a particularly striking example. Huaxi, like so many villages in the era of the Great Leap Forward and the Cultural Revolution in the 1950s and 1960s, struggled to feed its villagers; what distinguished it from the one million or so villages in China is its transformation in all aspects of life. In 2016, Huaxi's asset reached 53.5 billion rmb and the Huaxi Group owns 256 companies in China and the world in steel, textile, mining, offshore engineering, cosmetics, agricultural produce, and tourist industries; its average villager annual income was at 80,000 rmb, making it the wealthiest village in China.

Figure 1: Wu Renbao, center right, leading villagers to work, 1968

   Its charismatic leader, Communist Party Secretary from 1957 to 2013, Wu Renbao (1928–2013), led this transformation. Following the "land collectivization" in the 1950s, the Huaxi Village was formally established in 1961 with a population of 677. From 2001, Huaxi's economic achievement convinced 20 surrounding villages to join the original Huaxi to form a "Greater Huaxi Village" with a population of 35,000 and migrant population of 60,000. In 1969, Wu Renbao (figure 1) began a hardware factory (figure 2); its aim to make a profit from manufacturing was considered too "*bourgeois*" to be allowed to openly operate at the time. He and villagers evaded state inspections by shutting it down whenever inspectors arrived. The factory generated a considerable income. When Deng Xiaoping introduced the agricultural policy of "family responsibilities," moving away from Mao's great collectivization of land, Wu Renbao insisted on maintaining collective ownership of village land, and on collective agricultural and industrial production. His faith in socialist common ownership of land blended with the deep-rooted Confucianist tradition of the Great Sameness. Wu was curious about kibbutz in Israel and arranged his son Wu Xiedong to lead a research trip to Israel, although he realized that the kibbutz model could not be applied in Huaxi.[1] Wu gained deep trust of villagers by leading them to increase land productivity through merging small patches and developing a common irrigation infrastructure; he delivered

Figure 2: Huaxi Hardware Factory, 1970s

astonishing results in the increase of both agricultural production and the establishment of village industries. This development model in Huaxi provides villagers with social security while at the same time increases its market competitiveness, highly successful even though it does not fit into the dualistic conception of state-owned and private enterprises. [2]

Three architectural landmarks dominate the new village and defines its image. Towering over the greater Huaxi Village is the 72-story, 328 meter (1,076 ft) Longxi International Hotel, completed in 2011. It was meant to match—"in sync with the Central Government"—the tallest building in Beijing at the time of design,[3] and it is taller than the Eiffel Tower and the Chrysler Building, an immense landmark rising above the surrounding low-rise Chinese villages and farmland. Designed by the Shenzhen-based firm A+E Design, the Longxi Hotel is composed of three separate towers of hotel rooms (826 rooms in total) supporting a giant sphere of a restaurant and observation deck on top, a clear reference to the familiar figure of dragons playing with a pearl. The Oriental Pearl Tower in Shanghai comes immediately to mind as its precedent; the Longxi Hotel shapes its form closely following the tripartite body and the spherical top of the Oriental Pearl Tower. However, the figurative scheme of the Longxi Hotel is far more complex and vivid than that of the Oriental Pearl Tower; it has five "clubhouses"—special zones housing hotel public functions such as specialty restaurants, entertainment centers, and spa facilities—that recreate an idea of the "five elements" in Chinese cosmology: metal, wood, water, fire, and earth. Elaborately decorated, the most extraordinary centerpiece is the gold ox at the metal clubhouse on the sixtieth floor made of one ton of pure gold; real gold is used profusely throughout the building, including the bowls and chopsticks at the metal clubhouse. Its enormous banquet hall is large enough to host 1,600 dining guests, attended in part by special female entertainers from North Korea dressed in distinctive light blue Korean national costume. The entire building is clad with green reflective glass and colorful lights at night, announcing a massive and commanding presence in great contrast with the rural surroundings.

The group of nine pagoda-like buildings next to the Longxi International Hotel is equally striking. Each pagoda-like building is layered with nine roofs, topped with a golden finial, all in shades of reddish brown. Together, they form a square layout. These are common village buildings housing offices, a village hospital, and two residential towers for migrant workers in Huaxi who hold a bachelor degree or higher. Unlike the skyscraper that provided the Longxi Hotel with its architectural precedent, the Buddhist tower cluster seems to be the precedent for the nine-pagoda village center. At the center of this group of buildings are five pavilions set in the shape of the five stars on the Chinese flag, five marble statues of admired Chinese leaders (Mao Zedong, Zhou Enlai, Zhu De, Liu Shaoqi, and Deng Xiaoping), anchoring a series of statues of significant persons both from ancient Chinese history and from twentieth-century China. In the main pavilion there is a 145-ton bronze bell of the Huaxi Village. The entire complex is a distinctive hybrid, containing elements of a "central business district," a Buddhist tower cluster, and a parade of significant sculpted figures similar to Imperial palaces.

The third landmark building is the cultural and sports activities center shaped like an opened book. Built in 2016 on the site of an abandoned factory, this center contains a 2,500-seat conference center, a cinema, gym, recreation rooms, and indoor basketball, table tennis, and badminton courts. The conference center interior is modeled on that of the Great Hall of the People in Beijing.

Huaxi is inventing its architecture, and the leadership of the village chose to do it by having all, both Chinese and Western, both ancient and modern.

These three landmark buildings cradle a large square with a stage and a gigantic screen, a popular venue for evening dances. The central Huaxi village is linked together with public plazas, long corridors, and gates, all of which are covered with a large amount of images and Chinese characters promoting narratives of Huaxi's success (figure 3); these resemble those in imperial gardens such as the Long Corridor at the Summer Palace in Beijing but without the stylistic refinement. Huaxi is inventing its architecture and the leadership of the village chose to do it by having all, both Chinese and Western, both ancient and modern.

Figure 3: Narratives of Huaxi's success story displayed in the covered main entrance driveway

Surrounding the central Huaxi village are a series of theme parks—built for happiness and tourism—that include replicas of the Arc de Triomphe in Paris, the Tiananmen Square in Beijing, and a section of the Great Wall. The Village Museum is a replica of the main imperial buildings in Beijing's Forbidden City. The rest of the Greater Huaxi is made of uniform village houses, agricultural areas, and factories. While factories are similar to those in other parts of China, the village houses are designed loosely based on European styles, with just enough roof and elevation treatments to resemble features of European architecture. No particular stylistic distinctiveness is preferred, only a sense that villagers are rich enough to live in European-looking houses. Not intended in the design are almost universal adaptations of small patches around the houses for vegetables and herbs (cabbage, eggplants, tomatoes, spring onions), which are common for rural houses;

non-productive lawns associated with European houses are pointless to the villagers, it seems.

The success of Huaxi's social and architectural reality is a provocation to many of our normative assumptions of cities: property ownership, governance, urban design, regulation, spirit of place, and architecture. There is little doubt that the majority of Huaxi's population derive an immense sense of well-being and pride from this unique blend as a social and architectural construct. There is also little doubt that our normative theoretical frameworks of society and architecture are unprepared to explain this new reality. Is Huaxi Village not against the fundamental principle of self and family responsibilities that was at the heart of Deng Xiaoping's reform? Does Huaxi Village's architecture defy conventional wisdom of the importance of stylistic coherence and spirit of place? It is apparent that both the social form and architecture in Huaxi Village are strikingly simplistic and derivative, but these may be the surface events; the deeper framework of society and architecture of Huaxi presents us with an anthropological case study with meaningful architectural significance. The Great Sameness and group action, just like individualism, have an immensely complex variation that must be understood with deeper theoretical insight.

1
Ji Shuoming, *Belief (Xinyang)*, Beijing: Zuojia Chubanshe, 2018, p.22.
2
Xiaoshuo Hou, *Community Capitalism in China, The State, the Market, and Collectivism*, Cambridge: Cambridge University Press, 2013.
3
Ibid., p.140.

Corridors at Summer Palace
Beijing

Huaxi

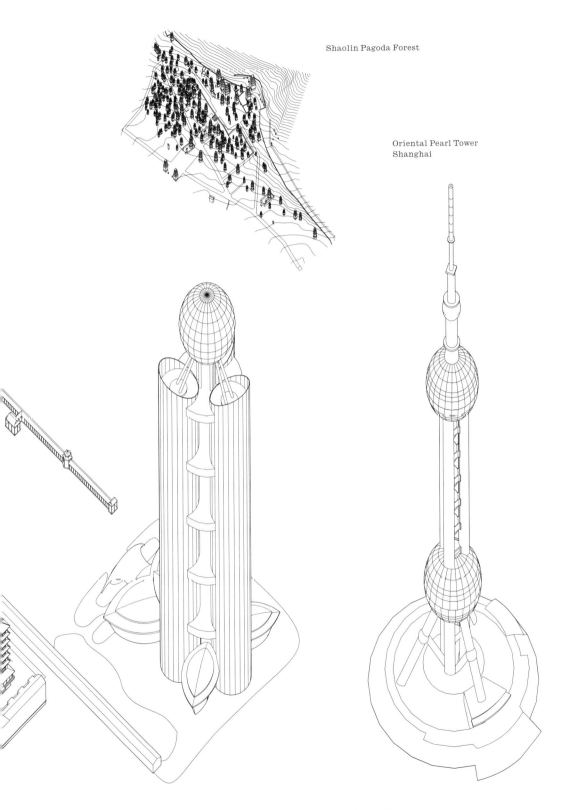

Shaolin Pagoda Forest

Oriental Pearl Tower
Shanghai

The Huaxi Collection: the Pagoda Forest, the Long Corridor,
and the Oriental Pearl Tower, scale 1:3,500

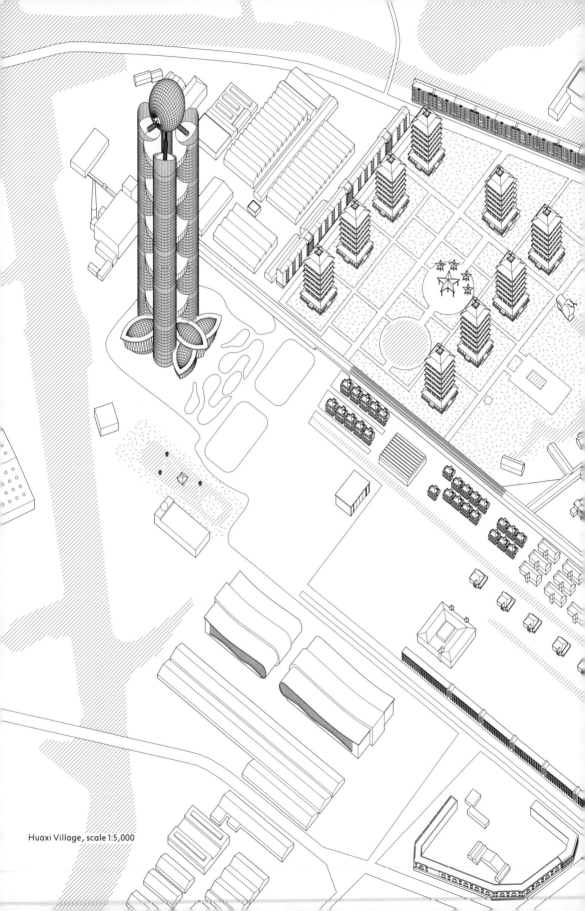

Huaxi Village, scale 1:5,000

1   The Longxi Hotel with its decorative lighting in the evening
2   Gold ox located at the Metal Clubhouse made of one ton
of pure gold
3   North Korean hostess in traditional dress
4   Entrance lobby of the Longxi Hotel, which houses a collection
of precious objects
5   An entertainment area themed after a village theater space in
the Wood Clubhouse
6   The Celestial Palace, a domed observation deck on the 72nd
floor of the Longxi Hotel
7   An artificial snow scene in the Earth Clubhouse
8   The Royal Chinese Restaurant on the 71st floor
9   The grand Banquet Hall with a capacity for 1,600 dinner guests

5

6

7

8

9

1

2

3

1   Reflective pool in front of the pagoda-shaped village buildings
2   Entrance to the village hospital, housed in one of the
pagoda-shaped buildings
3   Former training center for provincial cadre of Jiangsu
Province, this pagoda-shaped building is shown here in the
process of renovation
4   Sitting area in village square
5   A restaurant and a speciality shop at the ground floor of one
of the pagoda-shaped buildings
6   Statues of Mao Zedong, Zhu De, Zhuo Enlai, Liu Shaoqi, and
Deng Xiaoping overlooking the village square
7   Residents striking the 145 ton bronze bell in the village square
8   Entrance lobby to Huaxi Group Ltd., located in the central
pagoda-shaped building
9   Bird's-eye view of the village square

4

5

6

7

8

9

1

2

3

4

5

6

1 European-style villas
2 Ground view of European-style villas
3 Migrant worker housing with ground-floor shops forming the village barrier toward the north
4 Village houses
5 Pedestrian corridor system connecting the village houses
6 Residents socializing along the pedestrian corridor
7 Former residence of Wu Renbao, founder of Huaxi Village
8 Covered vehicular access invoking traditional Chinese long corridor designs with writings and paintings on beams forming narratives
9 Covered main entrance driveway, which also serves as an exhibition space of Huaxi's achievements
10 Huaxi Number Three Village
11 Evening dance at Longxi Square

7

8

9

10

11

Guangdong Province

Guangzhou

Guangzhou University City

Guangzhou new city center and Guangzhou University City, scale 1:100,000

Guangzhou University City: Spatializing the Group Intellect

The Guangzhou University City is an intriguing manifestation of what may be described as spaces for the
"group intellect," the intellectual expression of the Great
Sameness. It is the largest among China's university
cities. What appears to be a paradox—the university as a
space for diverse individualistic pursuit of knowledge now
reconstructed as uniformity—is in fact a logical progression of group action in the age of the competitive global
"knowledge economy." University cities in the traditional
European and American contexts meant natural communities built around a major university (Oxford, Cambridge,
Durham, Charlottesville) with their individual identities
constructed over periods of many centuries. Guangzhou's
University City was built in one go in nine months. The
Guangdong Province policy document adopted in 2001,
Development Planning of Guangzhou University City, speci-
fies the central role of the government in the planning and
construction of the University City; the parts played by
the ten universities eventually moved in were limited. The
document further explains the goal of this enormous development being the establishment of an integrated area of
education, scientific research, and academic exchange,
perhaps inspired by California's Silicon Valley. The policy
was published by the Guangzhou government on October
31, 2002, and at the same time, Zhang Dejiang (1946–), a
politician known for his ability to produce quick results,
became the Communist Party Secretary of Guangdong
Province, a position he held until 2007 when he was promoted to become a member of the Central Government in
Beijing. Located on Xiaoguwei Island in Panyu District
to the southeast of the city center of Guangzhou, with an
area of approximately 18 square kilometers and 8.9 million
square meters of floor area (not including the "urban villages"), the complex is capable of accommodating 37,000
residents and 180,000 students.[1] Construction began in
2003 three months after Zhang Dejiang took office, and
merely nine months later, ten universities moved into
the University City, a scale and speed of construction that
Zhang wanted to be seen as "a miracle." This was truly
remarkable considering the difficulty of purchasing agricultural land and relocating 14,000 indigenous villagers
living in 13 natural villages[2] who believed that they were

not compensated fairly, and the extraordinary archaeological finds during the process of construction.

Master-planned by one of China's leading architects He Jingtang (who also designed the China Pavilion for Shanghai's World Expo in 2010), the University City consists of three concentric rings and a radial road system, outlined by river channels forming part of the Pearl River Delta. This otherwise isolated island of delta sediment is connected with the city through one road tunnel, one underground train line, and two bridges. The inner ring is reserved for facilities shared among all universities such as a central lake, a sports stadium, an indoor cycling

One central issue here is, whether China's university cities manifest spatially a cultural conception of higher education in China, and whether this conception points to a future for China's higher education and research.

arena, and a center for literature and art. Living quarters are located between the first and second ring roads. The ten universities are located in the outer ring. A commercial southeast and northwest axis cuts through the entire University City, suggesting an axial link between the University City and the Guangzhou city center. Designed and constructed with great haste, the architecture of the University City is generically modernist. The Guangdong Science Center, opened in 2008, is perhaps most striking formally: a massive octopus-like structure that profits from the figures of a cotton tree flower (a tropical plant associated with Guangzhou), a sailing ship, a space ship, and an eye. It was designed by the Wuhan-based design institute CSADI. In 2012 SOM was hired to work with planners and village leaders to "humanize" the University City, which had been under intense criticism for lacking good functional planning, and for the sense of isolation for students and faculty. Like so many other rapidly constructed projects in China, the Guangzhou University City was a strategic fast and sweeping move—perhaps to establish the first-mover advantage—to be completed with successive improvements in the future.

The Guangzhou University City was Guangzhou's answer to China's first university city, the Oriental University City, opened in Langfang, Hebei Province in 2000. It invented a new way of turning agricultural land into profitable speculative urban use, adding to the existing developmental models of Central Business Districts, Industrial Zones, Science and Technological Parks, and Eco Cities, and it provided a solution to the shortage of university facilities at a time of rapid increase of university students. Within a decade, around one hundred "university cities" appeared in China.[3] All of them have strong components of real estate development within and around them; Shanghai's Songjiang University City in 2005 which houses eight universities, for instance, forms part of the enormous Songjiang new town development.

Current discussions on China's university cities are largely focused on the speculative real estate associated with their sites, as well as the lack of functional consideration resulting from their hasty design and construction. One central issue here is whether China's university cities manifest spatially a cultural conception of higher education in China, and whether this conception points to a future for China's higher education and research. For centuries, China had managed the education of its intellectual elite through a centrally administered examination system (figures 1 and 2); although dramatically different in form, China's attempt to create clusters of universities may have emerged precisely from this traditional conception of the progress of the scholar. The speed with which the idea of the university city caught on with municipal governments indicates more than just the promise of profit from real estate speculation. University cities in China incorporate both features of traditional university

Figure 1: Qiu Ying, *Releasing the Roll* (candidates gathering in front of the wall where results are released), c. 1540, detail.

Figure 2: Examination halls in Beijing in 1899. Photo: John Clark Ridpath

cities in Europe and America, and the economic logic of the concentration of the "creative class" in the knowledge economy as promoted in economic and social theories of Michael Porter and Richard Florida. Formation of manufacturing clusters in China has been proven to be successful in the past decades, but the formation of university cities as creative clusters is much more challenging. Despite their association with real estate speculation and their poor functional design, China's university cities open up two kinds of futures. One, this model accentuates the divide between academic communities and the society (town and gown) in that it undermines the efficacy of research rather than enhancing it. Second, this model dramatically speeds up team research and inter-disciplinary collaboration, and shortens the feedback loop in research, which leads to greater economic benefits and efficacy of knowledge.

With the hurried construction of university cities, China is clearly betting on the latter outcome. Its confidence comes from its tradition of group intellect management and from the logic of clustering in manufacturing. The culture of group action may indeed be the deciding factor in terms of the future success of this model of higher education. Perhaps the hardest task in this model is to sustain a degree of individual and institutional agency—and the moral and aesthetic lives associated with this agency—in the context of group action. Individual and institutional agency is the foundation for critical thinking and action that are central to cultural change. China's late

Qing dynasty in the 1800s gave us a vivid example of excessive uniform group action without criticality and change that contributed to a cultural decline. Understanding the nature of group action beyond its narrowest definitions is fundamental to both the acknowledgment of the force of a cultural logic and to the promotion of cultural change. Higher education is the most effective place to forge this continuity and transformation.

1
Data from *Detailed Control Plan of Guangzhou University City (Guangzhou daxue chengkongxing xiangxi guihua)* published by the government of Panyu, Guangzhou on May 26, 2015. This is a scaled down version of the original plan approved in 2001 that anticipated the University City to be twice as large and accommodating 350,000 to 400,000 people.

2
Zeng, Zhou, and Feng, *Xiaoguwei, Guangzhou*: Guangdong Education Press, 2014. Zhang Jiaying, and Tang Guohua, "An Exploration on the Construction of 'Heritage Trail' in Guangzhou University Town," *South Architecture*, February 2017, pp.117–22.

3
Li, Zhigang, Xun Li, and Lei Wang, "Speculative Urbanism and the Making of University Towns in China: A Case of Guangzhou University Town," *Habitat International* 44 (October 1, 2014): pp.422–31.

Cambridge
University of Cambridge

Oxford
Oxford University

Charlottesville
University of Virginia

The city as university, and the university as city
Scale 1:100,000

Durham
Duke University

Shenzhen University City

Peking University Shenzhen Graduate School, Tsinghua
University Shenzhen Graduate School, Chinese Academy of
Sciences Shenzhen Institute of Advanced Technology, Harbin
Institute of Technology Shenzhen, Southern University of
Science and Technology, Shenzhen University

Guangzhou University City

Sun Yat-sen University, South China University of Technology,
South China Normal University, Guangzhou University,
Guangdong University of Foreign Studies, Guangzhou
University of Chinese Medicine, Guangdong Pharmaceutical
University, Guangdong University of Technology, Guangzhou
Academy of Fine Arts, Xinghai Conservatory of Music

Songjiang University City

Shanghai International Studies University, Shanghai
University of International Business and Economics,
Shanghai Lixin University of Accounting and Finance,
Donghua University, Shanghai University of Engineering
Science, East Chian University of Political Science and Law,
Shanghai Institute of Visual Art

Guangzhou University City
Scale 1:20,000

1   Guangdong Science Center, located at the western tip of the island of Guangzhou University City
2   Guangdong Industrial University entrance gate
3   Guangzhou Velodrome on Central Campus
4   Museum of the Tomb of King of Southern Han (completed in 2019) located in the City Garden of the University City
5   Ancestral hall in Beiting Village
6   A mobile snack stand in front of an electric scooter shop in Beiting Village
7   Houses in Huishi Village
8   Library of South China University of Technology
9   Campus of South China University of Technology

5

6

7

8

9

The Architectural Profession

The Architectural Profession

The current European and American framework of professional practice, on which many other parts of the world modeled their own, is being reinvented in China. Cities were built for millennia without having any recognizable features of current professional practice. In its long history of constructing the environment, China began to embrace the European and American framework of professional practice in the twentieth century; by the end of the nineteenth century, its own building practice was no longer capable of meeting the functional, technological, hygienic, and material demands of building twentieth-century cities. More than one hundred years later, the architectural profession in China has internalized many technological and regulatory frameworks of professional practice; in the past four decades, the architectural profession in China vastly expanded their experience and expertise through building cities in shorter times, with greater functional complexity, higher technological aspirations, and at much larger scales than in the past. Like the building boom in America at the turn of the twentieth century, the building boom at the turn of the twenty-first century gradually transformed China's professional practice. China's Design Institutes are at the forefront of this transformation.

Design Institutes were never intended to be the laboratories for a new form of professional practice in China; they transformed themselves because of an existential crisis. In the early 1990s, the Chinese government, as part of market reform, gradually turned their non-essential "state-owned" institutions into institutions "responsible for their own profit and loss." This was not privatization, but creation of "state-owned market-operated enterprises." Confronted with the twin threat of an emerging sector of private architectural practices in China and the expansion of foreign design firms, and hampered by their reputation of conventional taste in architecture, design institutes went through a period of deep reflection and dramatic adjustment. However, their strong connection with the state—thus established access to resources and clients—have given them a distinct advantage in the Chinese cultural context. In the past four decades, they have remade themselves in several important ways. To address the innovation deficit, they have partnered with leading innovative architectural firms in the world as their local partner in China to build some of the most prominent buildings such as those for the Beijing Olympics and the Shanghai Expo. Through the formation of smaller design units within Design Institutes, they have allowed their designers to cultivate personal reputations as prominent architects. They have been able to consistently attract top graduates from leading Chinese schools of architecture by offering them important commissions and attractive and guaranteed compensation. They have leveraged on their capacity to provide reliable and high-quality service.

This experience of rebirth has encouraged China's design institutes to pursue a path of "all-in-one" professional practice. They firmly believe that size and innovation, state connection, and market flexibility, quantity and quality, speed, and competence are not mutually exclusive features of professional practice. They have given up the idea of the professional market of specialist consultancies by developing comprehensive capabilities in house. What this has effectively done is to have brought professional skills closer to each other: education, academic development, design, building and material science, construction, investment, and management. Many aspects of this model are being tested today: the limits of complexity and size, the extent to which it is integrated with academia, the strengths of connection with the state, and the level of comprehensive quality assurance. Would this foster a closer relationship between research and design that will alter the current dichotomy of innovative academia and conventional practice? Should PhD research in architecture be housed in design institutes instead of universities? TJAD (Tongji Architectural Design Group) is perhaps the most revealing example due to its size, experience, social prominence, and deep connection with one of China's leading centers for architectural education: the School of Architecture of Tongji University in Shanghai.

This "teaching hospital" version of architectural education, research, and practice has enormous potential for China and for many other parts of the world. Perhaps Europe's formation of the architectural profession was, and is, too deeply invested in the protection of experience and knowledge of the craft guilds; perhaps the proliferation of consultants in today's professional practice, as exemplified in the American context, has made the design and construction of buildings and cities far too fragmented and ineffective. Because of the fragmentation, innovation trapped in academia is difficult to be transferred to practice, and the quality of architectural practice, despite the increase of quantity, seems to have declined in this fragmented professional condition in terms of design and construction. China's Design Institutes, with all the challenges of evolving entities, test an alternative model of architectural professional practice that may indeed find a new balance between the efficacy of building and the intellectual insights of design culture.

Shanghai   Yangpu   Tongji Architectural Design Group

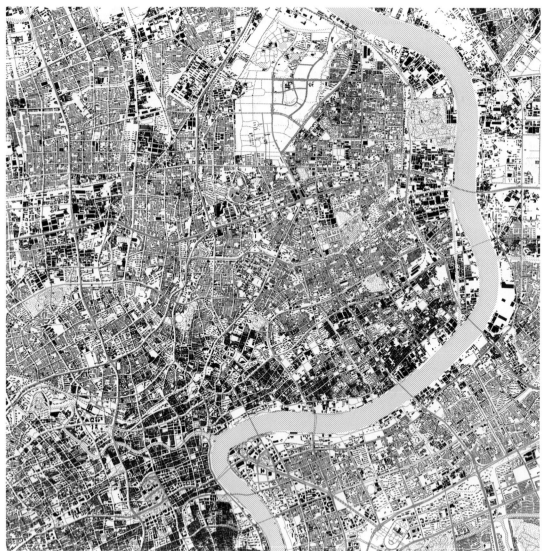

TJAD, Yangpu District, Shanghai, scale 1:100,000

TJAD:
Reinventing Professional Practice

Tongji Architectural Design Group (TJAD) is one of many large design firms (known as Design Institutes in China) that do the heavy lifting in architectural design for China's dramatic urbanization, even though internationally well-known architects dominate the headlines with their buildings in China. In addition, all foreign firms must partner with a Chinese firm, which develops construction details and documentation; for instance, Gensler partnered with TJAD during the contract and construction stage for the iconic 632-meter tall Shanghai Tower in Lujiazui. Established in the 1950s as part of the department of architecture of Tongji University, the modest operation has grown to have over 4,000 employees, who worked tirelessly to produce an impressive list of projects in China and, increasingly, in other parts of the world. TJAD designed the pioneering urban renewal project Xintiandi, the Main Pavilion and the construction of 138 national pavilions for Shanghai's 2010 World Expo, the prestigious Fangfei Garden of Beijing's Diaoyutai State Guest House, and the prominent Hangzhou Citizen's Center at Hangzhou's new city center. It was the designer of the African Union Headquarters in Addis Ababa in 2011, donated by China and built entirely with Chinese workers and construction materials. Their scope of work includes geological survey, architecture, infrastructure, landscape, construction, engineering, project management, urban planning, historic preservation, foreign contract, and a range of specialty designs. The headquarters, located just outside the campus of Tongji University, is evidence of its status: an enormous and elegant office converted from a bus depot in 2011, offering 65,422 square meters of office space. TJAD is one of the most attractive architectural design firms for aspiring young architectural graduates, capable of offering not only competitive compensation, but also opportunities to work on prestigious projects important for career advancement.

TJAD is an embodiment of the change of the architectural profession in China in the twentieth century. The professionalization of architectural practice was an idea introduced to China in the late nineteenth century by European powers following China's concessions to them as an aftermath of the Opium War (1839–1842). Prior to

Figure 1: Guan Songsheng (Kwan Sung Sing 1892–1960), founder of Kwan, Chu & Yang

Figure 2: Wang Jizhong discusses Shanghai Opera House Design with students in the 1960s, courtesy of Zhao Xiuheng

that, China's built environment was produced within an older craft-based tradition; the imperial version—known as Office of Works (*gongbu*)—was responsible for the production of architecture based on a strict hierarchical system. The post-Opium War opening of China resulted in an influx of foreign architectural firms such as Palmer & Turner Architects and Engineers, Atkinson & Dallas, and Moorhead & Halse; it also set forth the development of first private Chinese architectural firms such as Kwan, Chu & Yang (Jitai Gongchengsi) established by Chinese graduates from the MIT and University of Pennsylvania (figure 1).

The architectural profession was completely reorganized in China following Mao's victory over the Nationalists in 1949; private firms were abolished and architectural practice was modeled on the notion of "design institute" similar to that of the Soviet Union and Eastern Europe. Tongji Architectural Design began in 1952 as a "construction design bureau" affiliated with Tongji University; it was enlarged and renamed as "design institute" in 1958, and it existed until the start of the Cultural Revolution in 1968 when "architectural design" beyond civil engineering was seen to be too *bourgeois*. Architects who served the design group such as Feng Jizhong, Wang Jizhong (figure 2), and Huang Zuoshen (figure 3) also taught architecture at Tongji University. They worked on some of the first large-scale public buildings in Shanghai such as the 3,000-seat Shanghai Opera House (figure 4), and taught the first domestically educated architects of China. After 12 years of inactivity during the Cultural Revolution, Tongji Design Institute restarted in 1979, functioning as part of the Department of Architecture (figure 5). The post-1949 shift of China's profession of architecture from private practice to state-controlled design institutes was an ideological development. State involvement in architecture is certainly not unique; in the German and French cultural contexts for example, state projects have always been an important feature in the making of cities. The collectivization in China, the Soviet Union, and Eastern Europe of the architectural profession came as a complete replacement of private practice; the impact of this development is immense.

China and the Soviet Bloc headed toward very different directions following the momentous political changes in the 1980s. While the Soviet Union and Eastern European countries transitioned to become closer to the social and

Figure 3: Huang Zuoshen during a desk crit with a student in the 1960s, courtesy of Zhao Xiuheng

political model of Western Europe and the United States, China has kept its centralized structure and implemented a market regulated economic system. The majority of China's state owned enterprises took on the task of readjusting their operations to suit the marketplace while leveraging on their deep state connections.

TJAD went through this process in 1993, when it was incorporated into a listed company Tongji Science and Technologies, beginning its current status as a financially and legally independent company with strong ties with Tongji University. The architectural faculty of Tongji University continue to be involved with TJAD, and this complex network of architectural educators and professionals working in a competitive environment has produced a distinctive and viable professional environment. Teaching, research, practice, and financial gains benefited from this nebulous union. More than any other examples anywhere in the world, TJAD serves as the equivalent of a teaching hospital in architecture.[1] It has indeed

Figure 4: Model of Shanghai Opera House by Tongji University professors and students in the 1960s, courtesy of Zhao Xiuheng

Figure 5: Female architects of Tongji Design Institute in the 1980s, courtesy of TJAD

explored a new model of architectural practice with a tremendous potential for China and, with its increasing involvement with foreign projects, the world.

The most distinctive feature of TJAD is its large singular management structure; compared with its overseas rival and collaborator Gensler (more than 6,000 employees worldwide), TJAD reached its size by enlarging the professional activity to include all necessary services. TJAD is made of 16 subordinate institutes, two research centers, four branch firms in other parts of China, and is shareholder of nine architectural and graphic design companies. All of them share their resources internally. Rather than reproducing the cellular structure of a typical architectural practice in various locations as Gensler has done, TJAD swelled to its current size by grouping graphic design, interior design, construction drawing, project management, structural and building services design, and architectural design. This all-in-one approach, supported by their deep state and university connections, offers an enormous sense of security for potential clients; with high stakes in commercial and political projects, many large Chinese clients prefer to trust the all-in-one approach: TJAD is too prestigious to fail. TJAD, among other large design institutes, is able to guarantee quality with timely completion; they do not have to deal with the potential risks of engaging with a large number of consultants as is the norm for Gensler's multiple offices worldwide.

TJAD is changing the architectural profession. Traditional architectural practice is "design centric"; it is based on the idea that the design of architecture is the single most important "specialist" expertise where the value of architecture lies. This has been an idea that dominated the architectural profession from the late nineteenth century. Today, we are witnessing the antithesis of design centric architectural practice in the form of a "product centric" architectural practice; design-build companies offer well-tested formulas of architectural products in a marketplace where such products are all investors and shareholders need. Architecture as innovative design tends to be narrowed down to the media-ready images of iconic designs. This development to turn architecture into a financial instrument is committed neither to human life nor to the viability of the environment.

TJAD is genuinely interested in having both design centric and product centric capacities; it desires a balance of the two. This is a realistic goal in a cultural context in which having both is preferred, even though it is clearly a steep challenge. TJAD represents the best of the operation of the powerful "system" (*tizhi*); architects such as Wang Shu, Yung Ho Chang, Li Xiaodong, Zhang Ke, Atelier Deshaus, and Urbanus have articulated their positions as the "innovative other" outside the system. In response, TJAD has strategically collaborated with both leading Chinese architects and well-known foreign firms, developing its own capacity of cutting-edge designs. Compared with its counterparts such as Gensler, TJAD is far more active in organizing its own academic research due to its integration with Tongji University. Faculty teach and students intern through live projects. It has its own architectural journal, cultural salon, lecture series, and internal design competitions. TJAD, like all other design institutes, cultivates the prestige of their own designers. In 2014, out of 62 gold and silver medals awarded by the Architectural Society of China, six were given to TJAD.[2] If the Chinese intellectual framework of having both has led TJAD to bring together their "complete excellence" in a compelling way, it can certainly reformulate design innovation. "We specialize in everything," as one of its senior managers claimed without hesitation;[3] to specialize in design innovation is an entirely different realm of work that could indeed be TJAD's next ground of experimentation.

1
Zheng Shiling, "Architectural Design Practice and Disciplinary Reflection of University-affiliated Design Institute, A Historical Survey of Architectural Design Institute at Tongji University," *Time + Architecture*, June 2018, pp.19–21.
2
Wu Changfu, Tang Shouning, Xie Zhenyu, "The Cooperative Development of the Creation, Application and Research of Architectural Design, A Decade's Development of the Urban Architectural Design Institute, Tongji Architectural Design (Group) Co. Ltd.," *Time + Architecture*, June 2015, pp.150–53.
3
Interview conducted on May 29, 2015 by Michelle Stein, Sanyoon Park, and Jessie Zhang.

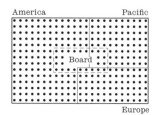

America   Pacific

Board

Europe

M. Arthur Gensler Jr. & Associates, Inc. 1985   Gensler, 1998

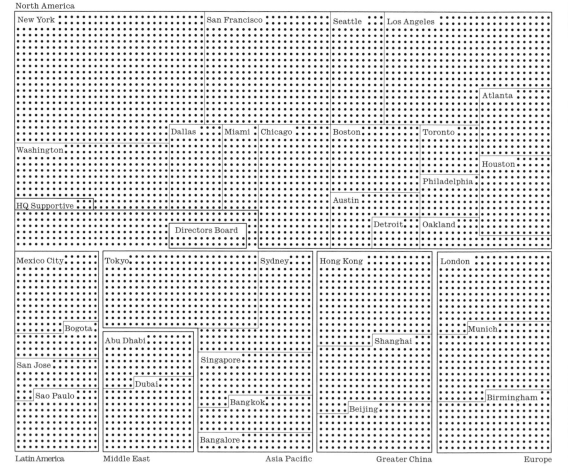

North America

New York   San Francisco   Seattle   Los Angeles

Atlanta

Dallas   Miami   Chicago   Boston   Toronto

Washington

Houston

Philadelphia

Austin

HQ Supportive

Detroit   Oakland

Directors Board

Mexico City   Tokyo   Sydney   Hong Kong   London

Bogota   Munich

Abu Dhabi   Shanghai

San Jose   Singapore

Dubai

Sao Paulo   Bangkok   Birmingham

Beijing

Bangalore

Latin America   Middle East   Asia Pacific   Greater China   Europe

Gensler, 2019

Two methods of scaling up the architectural firm:
modularity and hierarchy

Construction Design Bureau, Tongji University, 1953

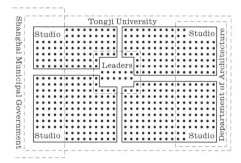

Architecture Design Institute, Tongji University, 1979

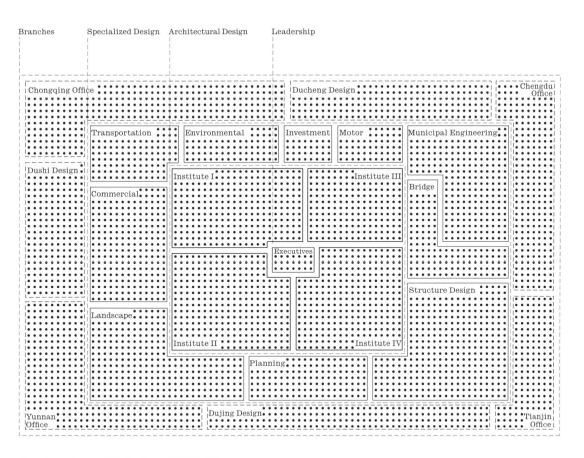

Tongji Architectural Design Group (TJAD). 2019

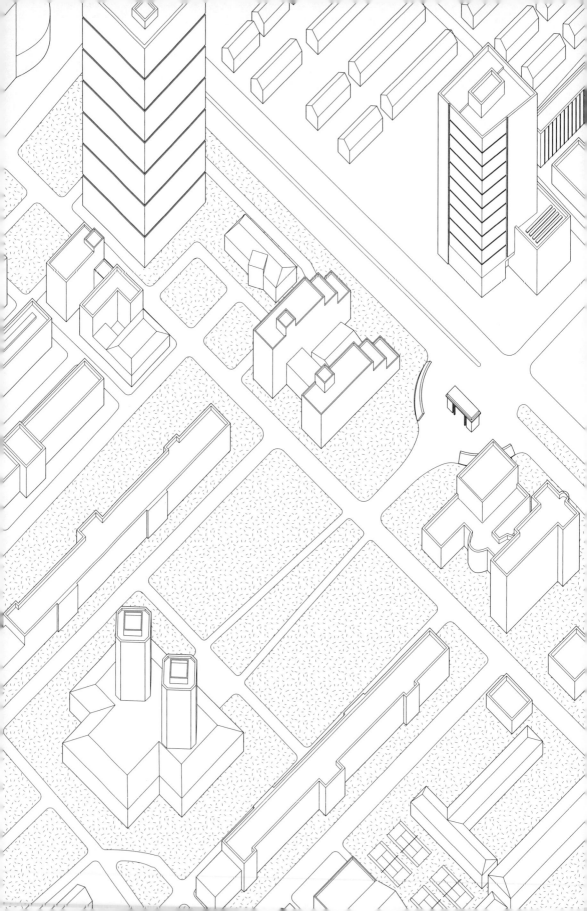

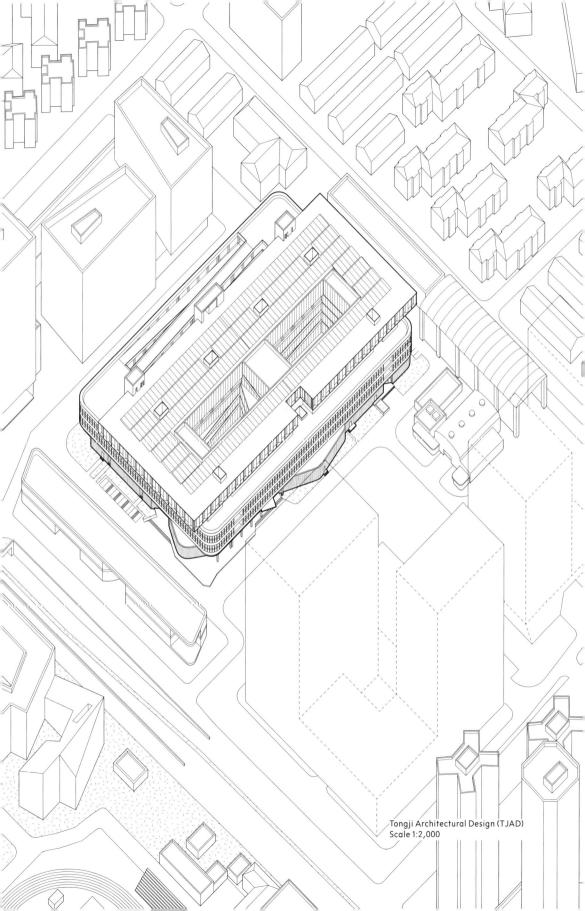

Tongji Architectural Design (TJAD)
Scale 1:2,000

TJAD Main Office Building

Completed in 1999, the office building was converted from a parking garage for a bus depot and takes advantage of its expansive spaces and the central void. Two floors were added to the additional structure. A connecting block inserted in the central void divides it into two courtyards, which offer natural light and access to the outdoors on several levels.

One of the two central courtyards

1/F
Lecture Hall
Cafe
Business Development Department
Meeting Rooms
Exhibition Hall
Dining Hall
Administrative Department
IT & Archives Department
Parking

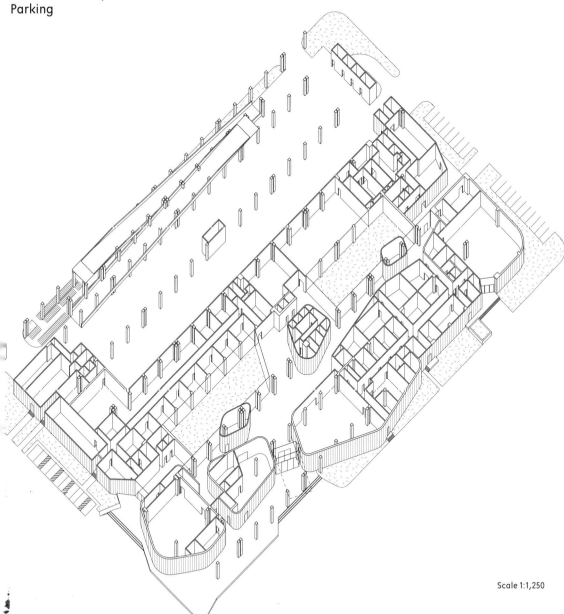

Scale 1:1,250

2/F
Municipal Engineering Design Institute
Tongchuang Architectural Design Institute
Tongli Architectural Design Institute
Rail Transit and Transportation
        Design Institute
Urban & Planning Design & Research Center
No. 1 Architectural Design Institute

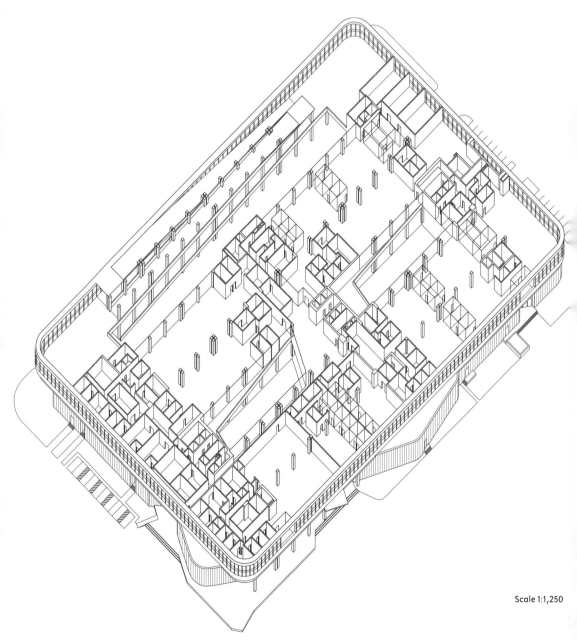

Scale 1:1,250

3/F
Ducheng Architectural Design Institute
No. 2 Architectural Design Institute
No. 3 Architectural Design Institute
No. 4 Architectural Design Institute

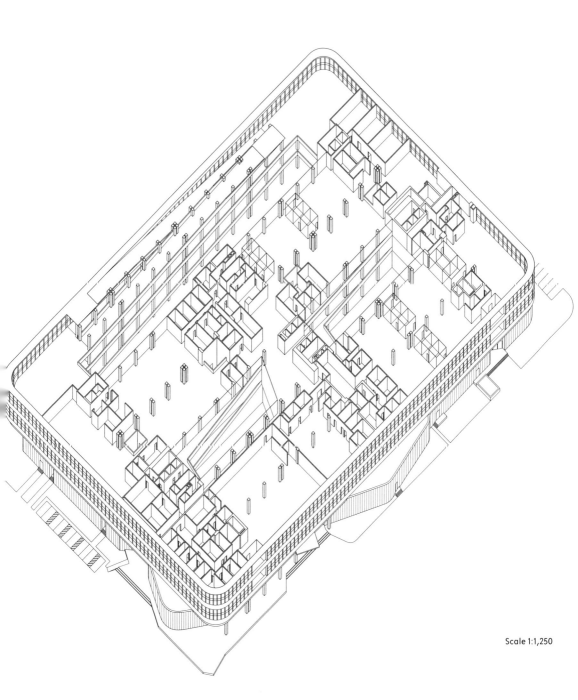

Scale 1:1,250

4/F
Landscape Design Institute
Tongyuan Architectural Design Institute
Bridge Engineering Design Institute
Traffic Planning Design Institute
Editorial Office of *Time + Architecture*
Urban Architectural Design Institute
Civil Engineering Design Institute
IT & Archives Department
Design Studios

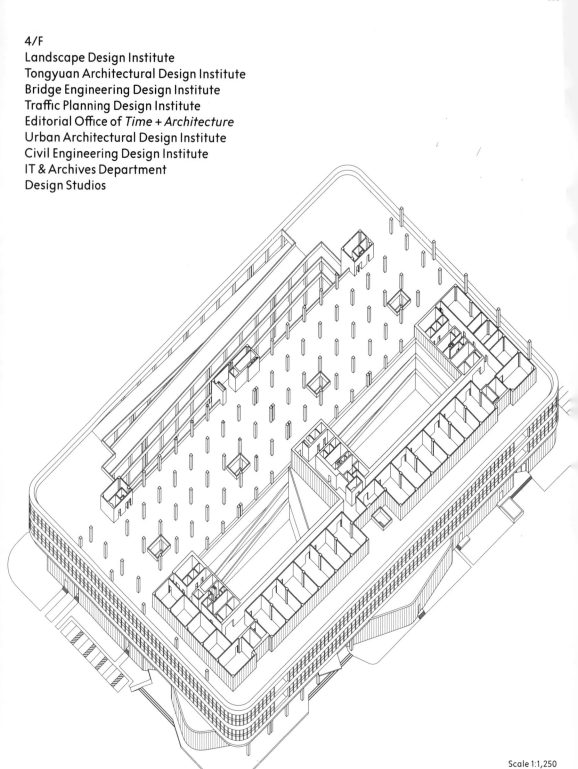

Scale 1:1,250

5/F
Tongpeng Architectural Design Institute
Dujing Architectural Design Institute
Fanya Architectural Design Institute
Project Management Department
Tongyi Architectural Design Institute
Engineering Investment Consulting Institute
TJAD Group Office Area
Technical Support & Quality Control
        Department
Technology Development Department

Scale 1:1,250

No. 1 Architectural Design Institute

No. 1 Architectural Design Institute is one of four main design institutes and a range of other specialized institutes. Each institute is organized like a mid-sized architectural office with complete professional design capacities.

Open studio space

Management and meeting spaces

Scale 1:500

1

2

3

1   View onto the exhibition space from the main entrance lobby
2   Live piano music during lunch break in the main lobby
3   Canteen
4   Ground floor, view toward entrance lobby
5   View from the fifth floor toward the city
6   Courtyard at ground level

4

5

6

Typological Drift: Emerging Cities in China is the second in the *Next Cities* publication series by UVA School of Architecture and its Next Cities Institute. The Next Cities series disseminates design research by faculty and students at UVA focused on the rapidly changing dynamics of global urban futures. The series expands on how design—in its theory and physical instantiation in the world—probes the questions and controversies of the day, continually writing new expressions of the city.

Authors:
Shiqiao Li and Esther Lorenz

Next Cities Series Editor:
Ila Berman

Graphic Design:
Neil Donnelly, Ben Fehrman-Lee, and Siiri Tännler

Managing Editor:
Jake Anderson

Published by Applied Research and Design Publishing, an imprint of ORO Editions.

Publisher: Gordon Goff
www.appliedresearchanddesign.com
info@appliedresearchanddesign.com

Copyright © 2021
Shiqiao Li and Esther Lorenz

10 9 8 7 6 5 4 3 2 1 First Edition
ISBN: 978-1-951541-71-2

Color Separations and Printing
ORO Group Ltd.
Printed in China

AR+D Publishing makes a continuous effort to minimize the overall carbon footprint of its publications. As part of this goal, AR+D, in association with Global ReLeaf, arranges to plant trees to replace those used in the manufacturing of the paper produced in its books. Global ReLeaf is American Forests' education an action program that helps individuals, organizations, agencies, and corprorations improve the local and global environment by planting and caring for trees.

Image Credits:

All illustrations in this book are the work of the authors Shiqiao Li and Esther Lorenz unless credited below or in the place where they appear.

Photographs:
p. 40, 41: Michael Peterson
p. 42, 43: Karilyn Johanesen
p. 45 (4): Seth Salcedo
p. 48: Michael Peterson
p. 59 (1, 5): Amelia Lin
p. 59 (2): Chris Weimann
p. 59 (3), p. 60 (3): Darcy Engle
p. 61 (7): Rhett Lin
p. 61 (8): Chris Weimann
p. 61 (9): Shannon Ruhl
p. 119 (8): Sangyoon Park
p. 121 (4–8): Donna Ryu
p. 213 (4,6): Karilyn Johanesen
p. 216 (1,2): Meng Huang
p. 217 (11): Meredith Blake
p. 250–251, p. 254 (1,2,4), p. 255 (5–8), p. 256 (2–4), p. 257 (5–8): Enze Huang, Zheng Meng, Tengxiao Liu
p. 290 (1,3,4), p. 291 (5–9): Gu Xueping

Drawings:
The illustrations on pages 199–209 are the work of Karilyn Johanesen, Meredith Blake, and John Devine from the 2016 UVA Architecture China Program taught by Shiqiao Li and Esther Lorenz.